S0-ATL-831

GREAT RADIO PERSONALITIES

In Historic Photographs

791. 44092

Anthony Slide

Dover Publications, Inc.
NEW YORK

CENTRAL LIBRARY

This book is for Rudy Vallee,
today, as in the past,
representative of the best in
American popular entertainment

Also by Anthony Slide

Early American Cinema (1970)
The Griffith Actresses (1973)
The Idols of Silence (1976)
The Big V: A History of the Vitagraph Company (1976)
Early Women Directors (1977)
Aspects of American Film History prior to 1920 (1978)
Films on Film History (1979)
The Kindergarten of the Movies: A History of the Fine Arts
    Company (1980)
The Vaudevillians (1981)

With Edward Wagenknecht

The Films of D. W. Griffith (1975)
Fifty Great American Silent Films, 1912–1920 (1980)

Frontispiece: **Burns and Allen:** George Burns (1896–   )
and Gracie Allen (1902–1964). Without question the greatest partnership in the history of vaudeville, radio and television, Burns
and Allen made their radio debut not in America but in England,
on the BBC, in June of 1929. They were first heard on CBS with
Guy Lombardo in 1932 and soon thereafter *The Burns and Allen
Show* became a radio perennial, making a happy transition to
television on October 12, 1950. One of the radio highspots of
1933 was Gracie's search for her supposedly lost brother, which
required that she pop up unexpectedly on any CBS program.

Copyright © 1982 by Anthony Slide.
All rights reserved under Pan American and International Copyright Conventions.

Published in Canada by General Publishing Company, Ltd., 30 Lesmill Road,
Don Mills, Toronto, Ontario.

Published in the United Kingdom by Constable and Company, Ltd., 10 Orange
Street, London WC2H 7EG.

Great Radio Personalities in Historic Photographs is a new work, first published by
Dover Publications, Inc., in 1982.

Manufactured in the United States of America
Dover Publications, Inc.
180 Varick Street
New York, N.Y. 10014

Library of Congress Cataloging in Publication Data

Slide, Anthony.
  Great radio personalities in historic photographs

  1. Radio broadcasters—Portraits. I. Title.
PN1991.4.A2S54   791.44′092′2   81-17347
ISBN 0-486-24298-6   AACR2

INTRODUCTION

"RADIO SWEEPING COUNTRY—1,000,000 sets in use": front-page headline in *Variety* (March 10, 1922).

Like that other great entertainer of mankind, the cinema, radio was not the result of one man's labors, but rather the end product of the pioneering work of various scientists, including James C. Maxwell, Heinrich Hertz, Guglielmo Marconi, Sir John Fleming and Lee De Forest. The commercial development of radio is generally credited to H. P. Davis, vice-president of the Westinghouse Electric and Manufacturing Company, which opened the first regularly scheduled radio station in the United States, KDKA in East Pittsburgh, on November 2, 1920. KDKA was quickly followed by WBZ in Springfield, Massachusetts, which opened on September 27, 1921; WJZ, which opened in Newark, New Jersey, on October 1, 1921, and KYW, which opened in Chicago on November 11, 1921. Commercial radio came into being on August 28, 1922, when WEAF in New York broadcast the first sponsored program.

American Telephone & Telegraph controlled the long-distance lines and thus controlled the growth of the radio network. However, in 1926, A. T. & T. sold its radio holdings, including WEAF, to the Radio Corporation of America, which already owned a number of stations, including WJZ, WJY in New York and WRC in Washington, D.C. From the Radio Corporation of America came the National Broadcasting Company, which in 1927 formed two networks from the stations owned by A. T. & T. and those owned by R.C.A. These two networks were named the Red and the Blue from the colors of the sheaths covering the network wires. That same year, 1927, the Columbia Broadcasting System was formed with a basic network of 16 stations in the Eastern United States. In 1943, NBC was required by the government to sell its Blue network, which it did to Edward J. Noble's American Broadcasting Company, and historic station WJZ was renamed WABC. The Mutual network had come into being in 1936 with the uniting of four local stations, WOR in New York, WGN in Chicago, WLW in Cincinnati and WXYZ in Detroit. The Mutual network was acquired in 1958 by the Hal Roach Studios.

Duston's Radio Log and Call Book for 1926 reveals that a typical radio station, WEAF in New York, broadcast an average of seven hours a day, excluding Sundays. To fill those hours performers were needed. First they came from the stage and the concert platform, introduced by anonymous announcers, and it was not until the late Twenties or early Thirties that radio came to develop its own stars. Interestingly, the evolution of the radio celebrity coincides with radio's domination of popular entertainment in America, taking over, as it did, a mantle previously worn by the motion picture and by vaudeville.

The link with vaudeville is a strategic one, for it was from vaudeville that the majority of radio's stars came. The "crude and congenitally amateur" radio programs of the Twenties that Robert Landry mentions in his 1946 book *This Fascinating Radio Business* were replaced by shows starring such major vaudeville figures as Al Jolson, Eddie Cantor and Ed Wynn. Brilliant young personalities such as Rudy Vallee were sounding the death knell for the likes of Harry Horlick and the A & P Gypsies. These new radio stars turned radio into nothing more than a glorified vaudeville show, just as they and others were to do with television in the late Forties and early Fifties. Supporting these new radio stars were radio's own peculiar creations, the countless announcers, so many in number that in 1937 *Variety* reported that about 150 of them a week moved from station to station. The marvelous thing about radio was that it encouraged vaudevillians to change and perfect their acts. The obvious example here is Fred Allen, probably radio's greatest star. It was Allen who succinctly summed up the success of the radio comedian as lying "in his ability to make the orchestra on his program laugh uproariously during the broadcast. Through hearing the background of guffawing in the studio the sponsor, listener, and average critic are all convinced that the comedian is a riot despite the fact that they can see nothing funny about the entire business."

Unlike today's network television, commercial radio provided more than merely comedy and music. It offered serious drama and music on a scale unequaled even by today's selection on public television. NBC could proudly boast of its symphony orchestra under the leadership of Arturo Toscanini. Orson Welles, Burgess Meredith, Norman Corwin and others were providing unsurpassed dramatic presentations. *Lux Radio Theatre* and similar programs offered adaptations of screen classics. In 1938, one could tune in to the Kate Smith program and listen to Lillian and Dorothy Gish in a 15-minute adaptation of *Orphans of the Storm,* while ten years later radio dramatized Malcolm Lowry's *Under the Volcano,* which to this day has proven too difficult a subject for the cinema to tackle.

Variety, the entertainment weekly, first reviewed a radio program on May 10, 1923, a musical show from the Capitol Theatre in New York, introduced by S. L. Rothafel (better known as "Roxy") and broadcast over WEAF. "Radio Reports" first appeared as a regular feature in *Variety* on January 7, 1931 (with reviews of Phil Spitalny and His Orchestra, Ted Lewis, Gus Van, the Finkenberg Hour, Pat Rooney and Son, and others), and that is as good a time as any from which to date the beginning of the golden age of radio. That golden age ended for radio when it was superseded as America's most popular form of entertainment by television in the early Fifties.

This volume offers rare photographs and capsule biographies (emphasizing the radio careers) of the great stars of radio's golden age. All the major figures are here, from the Happiness Boys and Vaughn De Leath to Frank Sinatra and Jack Webb. Aside from radio's major stars, I have tried to include a good sampling of those personalities whose time on radio is largely forgotten but who, hopefully, thanks to the very nature of the ether waves, are entertaining still the inhabitants of other galaxies out in space. To those privileged to have heard them, Johnny Marvin, Nat Brusiloff, Whispering Jack Smith, the Clicquot Club Eskimos and Edna Wallace Hopper are still held in affectionate memory. Not included are the majority of performers who starred in the various soap operas and mystery series, such as *The Romance of Helen Trent, Little Orphan Annie, This Is Nora Drake* and *The Lone Ranger*, because my feeling is that it was not the actresses and actors who

Jessica Dragonette on the Cities Service Concert (NBC) in the early Thirties, with Rosario Bourdon's orchestra and announcer Ford Bond.

Kay Kyser's show (NBC) in session, with Professor Kyser addressing the comedian Ish Kabibble.

Overall view of The Jack Benny Program *(NBC) in the early Forties, with Phil Harris leading his orchestra and, in the foreground, left to right, Benny, Mary Livingstone, Dennis Day, Eddie Anderson and Don Wilson.*

were stars but rather the characters that they portrayed. Everyone today knows the Lone Ranger and most people identify the role—an outrageous legal decision to the contrary—with television's Clayton Moore, but few will recall Jack Deeds, Earle Graser and Brace Beemer, all of whom portrayed the masked hero on radio.

My basic source for factual information on radio programs and radio personalities was the radio section of *Variety* from the Thirties through the Fifties. In addition, the following books were immensely helpful: *Treadmill to Oblivion* by Fred Allen (Little, Brown and Company, 1954), *The Big Broadcast* by Frank Buxton and Bill Owen (The Viking Press, 1972), *Tune in Yesterday* by John Dunning (Prentice-Hall, 1976), *There's Laughter in the Air* by John Gaver and Dave Stanley (Greenberg, 1945), *This Thing Called Broadcasting* by Alfred Goldsmith and Austin C. Lescarboura (Henry Holt and Company, 1930), *This Fascinating Radio Business* by Robert Landry (Bobbs-Merrill, 1946) and two volumes from the Thirties, *Who's Who in Radio* and *Stars of Radio,* both published with absolutely no indication as to their years of publication, their compilers or even their publishers.

The majority of photographs come from my own collection. For additional photographs and for help in researching the capsule biographies I am grateful to the Margaret Herrick Library of the Academy of Motion Picture Arts and Sciences, John Belton, Robert Bloch, Eddie Brandt, Robert Cushman, Bill Doyle, Robert A. Evans, Robert Gitt, Peter Hanson, Mike Hawks, Ronnie James, Richard Lamparski, David McCain, Al Rinker, Roger Robles, Herb Sterne, the Wisconsin Center for Film and

Theater Research and my editor at Dover, Stanley Appelbaum. Special thanks also to Vet Boswell, Norman Corwin, Dresser Dahlstead, Ralph Edwards, Alice Frost, Betty Garde, Lanny Ross, Arnold Stang and Ezra Stone. The Oscar statuette is the copyrighted property of the Academy of Motion Picture Arts and Sciences and the phrase Oscar is a registered trademark and service mark; both are used with permission.

A. S.

Notes:

(1) The frontispiece and the 235 illustrations in the body of the book are strictly portraits, whereas the three Introduction figures serve as background documents, offering fascinating overall views of popular programs in actual session.

(2) There is no index of the stars depicted because the arrangement of the book is alphabetical (aside from a number of very minor shifts to achieve a better page balance). A few pictures, however, show more than one star and only one personality per picture could be used as alphabetical anchor man. In the case of teams (such as Abbott and Costello), the first of the two names is used for alphabetizing. Here is the location, by picture number, of the other personalities whom it might otherwise be difficult to find (an asterisk indicates the presence of a capsule biography): Joseph Curtin (No. 90), William Daly (No. 214), Peter Donald (★; No. 71), Cliff Hall (No. 177), Phil Harris (★; No. 82), Alois Havrilla (No. 214), Portland Hoffa (No. 6), Benita Hume (No. 55), Tony Labriola (No. 164), William S. Paley (No. 213), Minerva Pious (★; No. 71), Jacques Renard (No. 53), Herb Shriner (★; No. 99), Penny Singleton (★; No. 132) and Don Wilson (★; No. 221).

GREAT RADIO
PERSONALITIES

In Historic Photographs

1. **Bud Abbott** (1895–1974; below) and **Lou Costello** (1906–1959). After many years in burlesque and vaudeville, Abbott and Costello were first heard on radio in 1938 as regulars on *The Kate Smith Hour,* on which the pair introduced their immortal "Who's on First" routine to the radio audience. Appearances with Edgar Bergen and as a summer replacement for Fred Allen followed, as did a Universal contract, which was to star Abbott and Costello in 35 feature films together. Between 1942 and 1950, Abbott and Costello had their own radio program, first on NBC and later on ABC. **2. Goodman** (1899–   ) and **Jane** (1905–1974) **Ace.** Goodman Ace was a Kansas newspaperman who, in 1928, married Jane Sherwood and entered radio with KMBC-Kansas City. The couple moved to Chicago in 1931 with their program titled *The Easy Aces* and it soon became a firm favorite on CBS, later moving to NBC and then back to CBS before it ended its run in 1945. Jane was the dumb wife and Goodman the ever-patient and happy-to-explain husband; she was known as the Mistress of Malapropism, coming out with phrases such as "We're insufferable friends," "Time wounds all heels" or "We are all cremated equal." The couple returned to CBS in 1948–1949 with a program titled *mr. ace & Jane,* sponsored by Army-Airforce Recruiting. Goodman Ace was responsible for the scripts for the shows and also wrote for Danny Kaye, Perry Como, Milton Berle and Sid Caesar as well as creating CBS's *You Are There.*

9583·5

4

3

3. Roy Acuff (1903–   ). Generally recognized as the King of Country Music, Roy Acuff is an accomplished singer, fiddler, bandleader and composer, whose best-known songs include "Wabash Cannon Ball," "The Great Speckled Bird" and "The Precious Jewel." Even before NBC network coverage of *The Grand Ole Opry* in 1939, Acuff was a regular on the program and, in time, became its greatest star. **4. Mason Adams** (1919–   ). Before becoming Charlie Hume on television's *Lou Grant,* Mason Adams was a major star of radio soap operas from 1946 through 1960, appearing on upwards of four live shows a day. He is best remembered as Pepper Young on NBC's *Pepper Young's Family* (1945–1959). **5–7. Fred Allen** (1894–1956). Vaudeville and revue star Fred Allen came to radio, with CBS, on October 23, 1932, in *The Linit Bath Club Revue. The Salad Bowl Revue* and *The Sal Hepatica Revue* followed before Allen hit his stride in 1934 with *Town Hall Tonight* (on NBC). In 1939, *Town Hall Tonight* became *The Fred Allen Show,* last heard on June 26, 1949. An intellectual in a radio world peopled by imbecile sponsors and network executives, Allen was forever feuding with his bosses, but, nonetheless, week after week turned out some of the best scripts heard on radio before or since. His autobiography, *Treadmill to Oblivion* (Little, Brown and Company, 1954), is a brilliant and humorous study of radio as seen through the eyes of one of the medium's greatest stars. In **6,** Allen is shown with his wife, Portland Hoffa, who acted with him. In **7,** he is seen with Jack Benny (see also No. 30 and Introduction figure). Their famous feud started in January of 1937 when Allen had a youthful violinist named Stuart Kanin on his program. The young lad played a difficult composition which led Allen to ad-lib, "Just imagine, this young man can play a piece perfectly that Benny can't even attempt after practicing for 40 years." Thus began a feud which was to become a national institution.

5

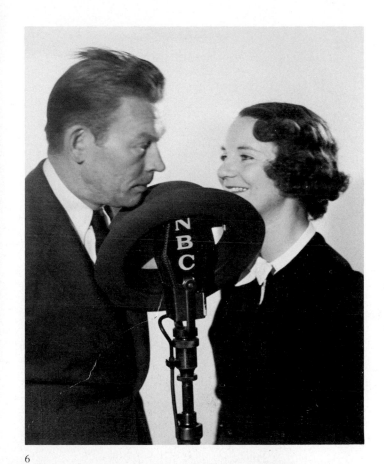

6

7

3

8

9

8. Mel Allen (1913–   ). The Voice of the Yankees from 1939 through 1964, Mel Allen was one of the top CBS sportscasters on both radio and television. In addition, when Allen first joined CBS in January of 1936 he worked as an announcer on such non-sports programs as *This Day Is Ours.* **9. Steve Allen** (1921–   ). Composer, author, pianist, comedian, actor, and for many years radio announcer: all of these titles fit Steve Allen, creator of NBC's *The Tonight Show,* PBS's *Meeting of Minds* and some of the best television programs of the past 30 years. Allen became an announcer on KOY-Phoenix in 1942, and in 1944 was to be heard in Los Angeles on KFAC and KMTR. He was a disc jockey on CBS in 1948, and thereafter moved on to films and television.

10

11

10. Fran Allison (1907–   ). Fran Allison entered radio in
Waterloo, Iowa, in 1934, as a singer and announcer, but it was
when she moved to Chicago shortly thereafter that she became
known to NBC listeners on *Smile Parade* (1938–1939), *Meet the
Meeks* (1947–1949) and, of course, *The Breakfast Club,* on which
she was a regular, as Aunt Fanny, in the Thirties and Forties. On
October 13, 1947, Fran Allison was seen for the first time, on
WBKB-Chicago, in *Kukla, Fran and Ollie* and remains an integral
part of that program to the present. **11. Don Ameche**
(1908–   ). After making his stage debut in Madison, Wisconsin, in 1928 and his New York debut the following year, Don
Ameche concentrated on radio work from 1930 until 1936, when
he left for Hollywood, appearing on *Betty and Bob, The First
Nighter, Grand Hotel* and *Jack Armstrong, the All American Boy,*
among many others, and all on NBC. After the start of his film
career, which lasted through the Seventies, Ameche still found
time for radio, appearing as a guest star and in the series *The
Bickersons* (NBC and CBS, 1946–1947).

13

14

12. Amos 'n' Andy: Freeman F. Gosden (at left in photo; 1899–   ) and Charles J. Correll (1890–   ). Gosden was Amos and Correll was Andy, white men playing blacks, on one of radio's best-loved programs, *Amos 'n' Andy,* first heard on NBC on August 19, 1926, and last heard in 1960. The two men began on radio in the early Twenties and developed their dialect comedy routines on WGN-Chicago in 1925. Although Gosden and Correll could not appear as the characters they had created in the 1951–1953 television series, they did supervise the programs. Al Smith was absolutely right when he said, somewhat testily, in 1939, "A large part of the American people were more interested in Kingfish, the beauty parlor and the Fresh Air Taxi Company [the chief components of the show] than they were in the affairs of their country." **13. Eddie Anderson** (1905–1977). One of the best-known black performers on radio, Eddie Anderson, as "Rochester," was a regular on Jack Benny's radio and television program from 1938 through 1964, asking that perpetual question in his familiar rasping voice: "What's that, boss?" In addition, Anderson was featured in more than 40 motion pictures between 1932 and 1963. (See also Introduction figure.) **14. Morey Amsterdam** (1912–   ). Morey Amsterdam, an excellent gag writer not to mention an expert cellist, began in show business in a musical-comedy act with his brother. He entered radio as a master of ceremonies on a local Los Angeles station in 1930, and later joined Al Pearce. Amsterdam was particularly busy in the Forties, having a regular series on WHN-New York, being a panelist on *Stop Me If You've Heard This One* on Mutual and having his own program, *The Morey Amsterdam Show,* first heard on CBS on July 10, 1948. Small wonder that Fred Allen once remarked, "The only thing we can turn on in our house without getting Morey Amsterdam is the water faucet."

15

15. The Andrews Sisters: (right to left) LaVerne (1915–1967), Patty (1920–   ) and Maxene (1918–   ). The Andrews Sisters started out in kiddie revues in Minneapolis in the late Twenties, and it was not until 1937 that they hit the big time with their recording of "Bei Mir Bist Du Schoen." Radio—*The Dole Pineapple Show*—followed, as did a record-breaking appearance at New York's Paramount Theatre. Their recordings of "Beer Barrel Polka," "Don't Sit Under the Apple Tree" and "Boogie Woogie Bugle Boy," among others, epitomize the Forties, when they were frequent guest stars on radio and had their own show, *Eight-to-the-Bar Ranch* (ABC, 1944), which became *N-K Musical Show* (CBS, 1946).

16. Eve Arden (1912–   ). A talented and versatile comedienne, Eve Arden became prominent on radio in the mid-Thirties on *The Ken Murray Program,* while also making a name for herself on stage. Films followed and then Miss Arden became a regular on *The Danny Kaye Show* (CBS, 1945) and *The Sealtest Village Store* (CBS, 1945–1948). On July 10, 1948, Eve Arden was first heard on CBS as *Our Miss Brooks,* the role with which she will always be associated, and which she also played on television from 1952 to 1956. Miss Arden was later seen on *The Eve Arden Show* (1957–1958) and *The Mothers-in-Law* (1967–1969) and continues to be active through the present.

17

18

17. Gene Austin (1900–1972). One of the most popular singers of his era, selling over 83,000,000 copies of his first hit, "My Blue Heaven," Gene Austin was a radio favorite for two decades, best remembered for his regular appearances on *The Joe Penner Show* from 1936 onward. Austin was also a songwriter, partially responsible for "The Lonesome Road" and "When My Sugar Walks Down the Street," among many others. *Variety* (May 3, 1932) described him as the "kingpin of the melody moaners when radio crooning was still considered away uptown."

18. Gene Autry (1907–   ). Aside from starring in 93 feature films between 1934 and 1953, popular cowboy singing star Gene Autry found time to appear for 16 years on his own show, *Gene Autry's Melody Ranch,* first heard on CBS on January 7, 1940. "Where the pavement ends and the West begins" was where Autry and his countless fans were to be found every Saturday or Sunday night, except for a period during the Second World War when Autry was busy elsewhere.

19

19. Mildred Bailey (1903–1951). Radio's Rockin' Chair Lady, Mildred Bailey was the sister of Al Rinker of the Rhythm Boys—she took her last name from her first and short-lived marriage to one Ed Bailey. Paul Whiteman was impressed by her style of singing and featured her regularly on his early broadcasts, and by 1939, Mildred Bailey was a regular on Camel's *Benny Goodman Show* on the NBC-Blue network, being held over when Bob Crosby and His Orchestra took over. *The Mildred Bailey Revue* was a popular CBS feature in the early Forties. **20. Olga Baclanova** (1899–1974). An exotic Russian actress who starred in a number of American films in the late Twenties and early Thirties, Olga Baclanova was heard from time to time on radio in the Thirties, particularly on *Olga Baclanova's Continental Revue* (1937), despite critics' complaints that her accent made it hard to understand who were her guests.

20

All the best from
Phil Baker

OF EVERSHARP'S
"TAKE IT OR LEAVE IT"

CBS
CBS
CBS

21

22

NBC

24

25

21. Art Baker (1898–1966). Art Baker gave guided tours at Los Angeles' famed Forest Lawn cemetery before entering radio as master of ceremonies on such shows as *Hollywood in Person* (CBS, 1937–1938), *People Are Funny* (1942–1943) and *Never Too Old* (Mutual, 1945). He was Bob Hope's announcer for a while and for 20 years, from 1938, hosted *Art Baker's Notebook* on KFI-Los Angeles. Beginning in 1951, Baker was master of ceremonies for television's *You Asked For It.*   **22. Phil Baker** (1896–1963). After appearing in vaudeville in partnership with Ben Bernie and in a series of revues in the Twenties, comedian-accordionist Phil Baker gained his first major radio exposure thanks to Rudy Vallee. In 1933, he was given his own radio program as *The Armour Jester* on the NBC-Blue network, and he continued to star on his own show through 1938. In 1939, Baker was featured in *Honolulu Bound* on CBS, and in 1941 he took over as host of the CBS quiz show *Take It or Leave It,* with which Baker remained through 1947. He retired in 1955 and moved with his Danish-born wife to Copenhagen, where he died.   **23. Kenny Baker** (1912–). A pleasant, good-looking performer with a rich tenor voice,

Kenny Baker made his professional radio debut in 1930 on a Long Beach, California, station. Jack Benny heard him at Los Angeles' Cocoanut Grove and brought Baker onto his program in 1935. After his appearances on *Pabst's Blue Ribbon Town* in 1943, Baker was voted radio's number-one tenor of 1944. He made frequent guest appearances on various shows and was also heard regularly on ABC's *Glamor Manor* in the Forties.   **24. Lucille Ball** (1910–). A film comedienne from the mid-Thirties onwards, Lucille Ball became popular on radio in the Forties as a guest performer and as the star of *My Favorite Husband* (CBS, 1948–1951). Her television series *I Love Lucy* (CBS, 1951–1961) was also heard on radio for a time.   **25. Smith Ballew** (1902–). A good-looking singer and bandleader, Smith Ballew had played with Ted Fio Rito, Ben Pollack and Freddie Rich before forming his own orchestra for vaudeville and nightclubs. He was featured on many radio programs and, in 1936, took over from Al Jolson as host of *Shell Chateau,* opening the program with "Tonight There Is Music in the Air" and closing it with "Home."

26. Tallulah Bankhead (1902–1968). One of the major theatrical personalities of this century, of whose voice Fred Allen said it was like a man pulling his foot out of a pail of yogurt, Tallulah Bankhead made her radio debut with Rudy Vallee on February 15, 1934. She was to be a frequent guest star on Vallee's show as well as on *Time to Smile* (NBC, 1941), *The Raleigh Room* and *The Fred Allen Show,* on which, on October 27, 1946, she and Allen performed the classic skit "The Mr. and Mrs. Breakfast Broadcasting Satire." Tallulah Bankhead was the star of the last major variety program on radio, NBC's *The Big Show* (1950–1952). **27. Pat Barrett** (1887–1959). Pat Barrett, former farmer and vaudevillian, was radio's Uncle Ezra, first heard on WTMJ-Milwaukee in 1929, and a year later moving to WLS-Chicago. He had his own show on NBC in the Thirties and Forties, supposedly originating from the rural Rosedale Station E-Z-R-A, and was also a favorite on *The National Barn Dance.* **28. André Baruch** (1906–   ). French-born André Baruch came to the United States at the age of 13 and became one of the more familiar voices on radio, a commercial spokesman for Lucky Strike for 22 years and the voice for U.S. Steel. Baruch was announcer for Kate Smith, Stoopnagle and Budd and, of course, *Your Hit Parade,* which began on NBC in the spring of 1935. With his wife, Bea Wain, Baruch is still to be heard on radio.

26

27

28

29. William Bendix (1906–1964). William Bendix, whose screen career as a likeable tough guy spanned the years from 1942 until his death, came to radio in 1943 with *The Life of Riley* on NBC. Chester A. Riley was initially played on television in 1950 by Jackie Gleason and the show was promptly canceled, but in 1953 William Bendix brought the character back and continued to play him until 1958; the radio program had ended in 1951. **30. Jack Benny** (1894–1974). Vaudeville and early talkies made Jack Benny a star, but it was radio that kept him a star. He made his radio debut on the Ed Sullivan program on March 29, 1932, and, as a result, was signed as master of ceremonies for *The Canada Dry Ginger Ale Program* on NBC. Jack Benny remained the star of the shows that followed, but the titles changed with the sponsors: *The Chevrolet Program,* beginning March 3, 1933, *The General Tire Program,* beginning April 6, 1934, *The Jello Program,* beginning October 14, 1934, *The Grape Nuts Program,* beginning October 14, 1942, and *The Jack Benny Program,* beginning October 1, 1944 (all NBC). Benny moved to CBS on January 2, 1949, and his radio program was last heard on May 22, 1955, making a magnificent total of 924 shows in 23 years. (See also No. 7 and Introduction figure.)

29

30

31

31. Gertrude Berg (1899–1966). Gertrude Berg gained lasting fame as the Jewish matriarch Molly Goldberg, star of *The Rise of the Goldbergs,* which Mrs. Berg also wrote, and which was heard, not always continuously, from 1929 through 1945, first on NBC and later on CBS. After its success on television in 1949, it returned to CBS radio for a season. Gertrude Berg was a prolific writer, turning out more than 15,000,000 words during her career, and, in addition to *The Goldbergs,* wrote and starred in *House of Glass* (NBC, 1934) and also wrote *Kate Hopkins, Angel of Mercy* (CBS, 1940–1943). In addition, Gertrude Berg found time to bring the Goldberg family to vaudeville, to the Broadway stage in *Molly and Me* (1948) and to the printed page with *The Rise of the Goldbergs* (1931) and *The Molly Goldberg Cookbook* (1955); Mrs. Berg also appeared in other stage roles, notably as Mrs. Jacoby in *A Majority of One* (1959). Brooks Atkinson summed up the secret of the appeal and success of this remarkable woman when he wrote, "Mrs. Berg is a real human being who believes in the people she writes about and is not ashamed of their simplicity." **32. Edgar Bergen** (1903–1978). The extraordinary thing about Edgar Bergen is that he managed to make a name for himself as a ventriloquist on radio, with his best-known dummies being Charlie McCarthy and Mortimer Snerd (first introduced November 1939). Bergen made radio audiences laugh from 1936, when he appeared as a guest of Rudy Vallee, through 1956. *The Charlie McCarthy Show,* as it was titled, was first heard on NBC, under the sponsorship of Chase and Sanborn, on May 9, 1937. Chase and Sanborn, NBC and Bergen parted company in 1948, and thereafter the ventriloquist was heard on CBS under the sponsorship of Coca Cola, Richard Hudnut, Lanolin, Chicken of the Sea and Kraft. (See also No. 71.)

33

34

33. Milton Berle (1908–   ). He might have been Mr. Television, but Milton Berle was also remarkably active in radio, although never as successful as he was to be on television. Berle was featured on *Stop Me If You've Heard This One* (NBC, 1939), *Three-Ring Time* (Mutual, 1941), *Let Yourself Go* (NBC-Blue, 1944) and *The Milton Berle Show* (NBC, 1947). He had made his radio debut in 1934 after serving time in vaudeville and clubs.

34. Ben Bernie (1891–1943). After working in vaudeville with Phil Baker, Ben Bernie, the Old Maestro, took over a band and brought it to a local New York radio station in 1923. Thanks to a long-running feud with Walter Winchell, Bernie's name became known to millions of radio listeners, and he was to be heard on his own network programs from 1931 until his death. Bernie was a colorful personality, noted for the intimate manner of his comments, his fat cigars and his catchphrase, "Yowsah, Yowsah, Yowsah."

36

35

on his program, and he will always be remembered for the characters of Monsieur Le Blanc, Sy the Mexican Gardener, the Maxwell Automobile and, of course, the railroad conductor announcing, "Ana-heim, A-zusa and Kook-amunga." In addition, Blanc was kept busy on dozens of other radio programs, too numerous to mention. **36. Irene Bordoni** (1895–1953). The French-born entertainer noted for her saucy songs and the manner in which she rolled her big eyes had already been a successful star of vaudeville, musical comedy and revue before commencing her radio career in 1931 as the Coty Playgirl. Miss Bordoni was a guest singer on many variety programs as well as being featured on *The RKO Hour*.

35. Mel Blanc (1908–   ). Blanc made his radio debut with KGW-Portland in 1927, but it was not until 1931, when he was on Portland's KEX, that he began to get a reputation for the voices that he could create. On May 22, 1934, *Variety* published a rave review of Blanc's *Cobwebs and Nuts* program on KEX. In 1937, Blanc became a regular on the Johnny Murray show out of KFWB-Los Angeles, and that same year signed a contract with the Warner Bros. cartoon department, for whom he was to create the voices of Bugs Bunny, Daffy Duck, Tweetie Pie, Porky Pig and countless others. Blanc joined Jack Benny in 1940 as a regular

37

38

"Around and around she goes, and where she stops nobody knows," intoned Major Bowes each week as he spun the wheel of fortune on his amateur hour, heard from 1934 until the Major's death, first on NBC and later on CBS. Major Bowes had already retired, a wealthy and successful man, in 1905, but the San Francisco earthquake and fire of the following year wiped out his fortune. He soon started building a second fortune in real estate, opening, in 1918, New York's Capitol Theatre, from which he broadcast his first radio program, *Major Bowes' Capitol Family Hour,* a regular Sunday morning feature on CBS until May of 1941. **40. The Boswell Sisters:** (left to right) Martha Meldania Boswell (1905–1958), Constance Foore Boswell (1907–1976) and Helvetia George Boswell (1911–   ). On March 18, 1931, *Variety* wrote of the Boswell Sisters, "They qualify as a utility turn that can fit into various spots." And there lay the secret of the Boswell Sisters' success on radio in the Thirties. Martha and Connie had won an amateur radio contest as early as 1922, and the three sang together on WSMB-New Orleans in the mid-Twenties (contrary to all published reports, the sisters were not born in New Orleans). During 1929 and 1930, the Boswells were in Los Angeles, singing on KFWB, and in February of 1931 signed with NBC in New York to appear on *Pleasure Hour.* They moved to CBS in June of 1931, and got their first commercial sponsor, Baker Chocolate, in October of that year. During 1932, the Boswell Sisters were to be heard on *Music That Satisfies,* while in 1934 they co-starred with Bing Crosby on *The Woodbury Hour.* European appearances and vaudeville tours followed until 1936 when Vet retired to have a child and the group broke up. Connie had married the trio's manager, Harry Leedy, in 1935 and continued as a solo act through the Fifties. There were many other sister acts singing on radio in the Thirties, including the Brox Sisters, the Pickens Sisters and the Three X Sisters, but none achieved the lasting fame on radio or record of the Boswells.

37. Victor Borge (1909–   ). Borge made his debut as a professional concert pianist in his native Denmark at the age of ten. He came to America in 1940, when the Nazis overran Europe and, in December of 1941, appeared as a guest star on Bing Crosby's *Kraft Music Hall.* He remained with the show for the next 56 weeks. Early in 1943, Borge had his own five-minute radio show, for M-G-M, Mondays through Fridays, on the NBC-Blue network, and was then given the first major program of his own as a summer replacement for Fibber McGee and Molly. Borge made his American concert debut in 1945, but it was not until 1953 that he began giving the one-man shows for which he is so well known. **38. Bob and Ray:** Bob Elliott (at left in photo; 1923–   ) and Ray Goulding (1922–   ). As *The New Yorker* (September 24, 1973) commented, Bob and Ray are "known in every swinging American household." Comedians in the tradition of Stoopnagle and Budd, they have created such memorable characters as T. Wilson Messy, Wally Ballou, Calvin L. Hoogevin, Webley Webster, Chester Harbrouck Frisbie and Mary McGoon. Bob made his radio debut in 1941, Ray in 1936, and the two first came together in 1946 on WHDH-Boston, where both were staff announcers. They have been broadcasting together ever since. **39. Major Edward Bowes** (1874–1946).

39

40

41

42

41. William Boyd (1895–1972). William Boyd had been a popular leading man in silent films before becoming the screen's Hopalong Cassidy in 1934. Boyd brought Hopalong Cassidy to radio, on CBS, on Monday, August 11, 1941, and critics were quick to note that the program was obviously modeled after *The Lone Ranger*. Boyd enjoyed even greater popularity as the Western hero on the Mutual radio series of the Fifties. **42. Tom Breneman** (1902–1948). With the announcement, "I'm Tom Breneman, now you can *all* applaud," Breneman would commence his immensely popular *Breakfast in Hollywood* program, which was heard over ABC every weekday morning at eight o'clock. Breneman would indulge in fast comic repartee with his female guests, sport a woman's hat and, quite often, put a middle-aged housewife over his knee and spank her. Women loved it, and flocked to the restaurant that Breneman owned (it was from there the show emanated) on Vine Street in Hollywood. *Breakfast*

in Hollywood was first broadcast, on the NBC-Blue network, as *Breakfast at Sardi's*, coming from the Hollywood restaurant of that name, in 1941. After a vaudeville career as a song-and-dance man, Breneman became popular on local radio in 1930, performing "Tom and Wash" sketches on KFWB in Los Angeles. Other programs, such as *Answer Auction* on CBS (1940), followed. At the time of his death, *Breakfast in Hollywood* was still running, and Breneman was regarded as one of radio's favorite personalities, heard over 220 stations. **43. Fannie Brice** (1891–1951). A star of the *Ziegfeld Follies* and vaudeville, Fannie Brice created one of radio's beloved characters, Baby Snooks (seen in the photo), on the radio version of the *Follies* on February 29, 1936. Neither Miss Brice nor Baby Snooks (with her famous simpering question, "Why, daddy?") was away from radio for the next 15 years until death put an end to the entertainer's career just as she was considering retirement.

44

44. Norman Brokenshire (1898–1965). With his folksy greeting of "How do you do, ladies and gentlemen, how do you do," Norman Brokenshire became one of the great announcers of early radio, beginning with WJZ in the early Twenties and covering the presidential inaugurations of Coolidge (1925) and Hoover (1929). Alcohol was responsible for the demise of his career in 1934, but thanks to Alcoholics Anonymous he made a magnificent recovery, and returned to network radio as announcer for U.S. Steel's *Theatre Guild on the Air* in 1945. **45. Billie Burke** (1885–1970). A light comedienne on stage (from 1898) and in films (from 1915), Billie Burke was a frequent radio guest in the Thirties and Forties and also had her own show on CBS from 1944 through 1946.

45

46

46. Nat Brusiloff (circa 1904–1951). A concert performer at the age of five, composer–musician Nat Brusiloff became house conductor for CBS in 1929, working with Kate Smith, the Boswell Sisters, Morton Downey, Bing Crosby and others. Brusiloff moved to WMCA in 1933, and was noted not only for his music but also his comedy songs. A top radio orchestra leader of the Thirties, Nat Brusiloff remained active until his death.

48

49

47. Bob Burns (1890–1956). Bob Burns was radio's philosophical humorist—similar in style to Will Rogers—who told of his relatives in the Ozarks and played a musical instrument of his own invention, the bazooka. As an NBC release once stated, "His stuff has the freshness and vigor of an Arkansas breeze." Burns began his professional career in vaudeville in 1911, and entered radio in 1932. After several years with Bing Crosby on *The Kraft Music Hall,* Burns was given his own show, initially titled *The Arkansas Traveler,* on CBS, in 1941, sponsored by Campbell's Soups, which ran until 1947 when Burns retired. **48. Dr. S. Parkes Cadman** (1864–1936). The noted Brooklyn Congregational minister and syndicated columnist Samuel Parkes Cadman was a pioneer of religious broadcasting in the United States with his own Sunday series, *The National Radio Pulpit,* on NBC from the mid to the late Twenties. English-born Cadman was also the author of *Charles Darwin and Other English Thinkers* (1916), *The Lure of London* (1925) and *Adventure for Happiness* (1935). **49. Cab Calloway** (1907–   ). Cab Calloway was probably the only black orchestra leader to be heard coast-to-coast on network radio in the Thirties. In 1941, he hosted *Cab Calloway's Quizzical* on WOR, which was billed as Harlem's own idea of what a musical quiz should be.

50

51

50. Judy Canova (1916–). Judy Canova was the hillbilly canary, once described as Arkansas' answer to Beatrice Lillie and Oklahoma's answer to Fannie Brice, although she was actually born in Florida. Judy Canova came to radio from vaudeville and films, and began her own show on CBS in the summer of 1943; it moved to NBC the following year and was to be heard through 1953. **51. Jack Carson** (1910–1963). A nightclub entertainer with a song-and-dance act, who began in vaudeville, Jack Carson became the affable fall guy of radio and films. He was featured in *The Signal Carnival* (1941), *The Jack Carson Show* (1943–1947), *Camel Comedy Caravan* (1943) and *The Sealtest Village Store* (1947–1948), all on NBC.

52

52 & 53. Eddie Cantor (1892–1962). A brilliant comedian and an all-round entertainer who had become a major star from his appearances in the *Ziegfeld Follies,* vaudeville and musical comedies such as *Kid Boots* and *Whoopee!,* Eddie Cantor was a natural for radio, and his show, which began on NBC in 1931 and continued through 1949, was one of the medium's most popular. Cantor was first heard on radio in the early Twenties, but his first major triumph was as a guest on *The Fleischmann Hour* on February 5, 1931. In **53** he is seen with Rubinoff (see No. 194) and Jacques Renard (violinist, bandleader, music director) on *The Texaco Hour,* December 29, 1948.

53

61

61. Norman Corwin (1910–   ). Writer, director and producer Norman Corwin was one of the most talented and creative men on radio, a writer who recognized the potential of radio drama. In 1942, Carl Van Doren wrote, "Though other writers besides Norman Corwin have written plays to be broadcast on the air, and good ones, he stands out as an accomplished, acknowledged master. He is to American radio what Marlowe was to the Elizabethan stage." Corwin came to the medium reading nightly news commentaries on WBZA and then introduced dramatized poetry readings, *Poetic License,* on WQXR in 1937. He is best known for his CBS series in the early Forties, *By Corwin, This is War, An American in England* and *Columbia Presents Corwin.* In the photo he is giving the radio cue for "Keep that level of sound."

62

• **62. Jesse Crawford** (1896–1962). Known as "The Poet of the Organ," Jesse Crawford was probably the best known of radio organists, initially broadcasting over CBS on *The Paramount-Publix Hour*, originating from New York's Paramount Theatre, where Crawford and his wife had been resident organists since it opened in 1926. **63. Bing Crosby** (1903–1977). Harry Lillis Crosby, Jr. made his radio debut in 1930 and the following year had his own 15-minute program on CBS. Crosby is best known on radio as the star of *The Kraft Music Hall* (1935–1946) and as the man largely responsible for the introduction of prerecorded programs to network radio. In addition to radio work through the Fifties, followed by many television appearances, Crosby starred in more than 50 feature films between 1932 and 1966.

63

64

65

64. Xavier Cugat (1900–   ). Born in Spain and raised in Cuba, Xavier Cugat came to New York at the age of 12. He founded his own Latin combo in 1928, and in 1931 created his first big band, becoming known as "The Man Who Made America Rumba-Conscious." Cugat is best known on radio for Camel's *Romance and Rumbas* (NBC, 1941) and *The Xavier Cugat Show* (NBC-Blue, 1943), sponsored by Dubonnet, which em-phasized that "both are products of the U.S.A." **65. Bill Cullen** (1920–   ). Bill Cullen has never stopped working on radio or television since he joined WWSW-Philadelphia in 1939. In 1944, Cullen joined CBS in New York as a staff announcer; on that network he is known for *Casey, Crime Photographer* (1948–1949) and *Hit the Jackpot* (1948–1949), and on others for *Quick as a Flash* (ABC, 1949) and *This Is Nora Drake* (NBC, 1949–1959).

66

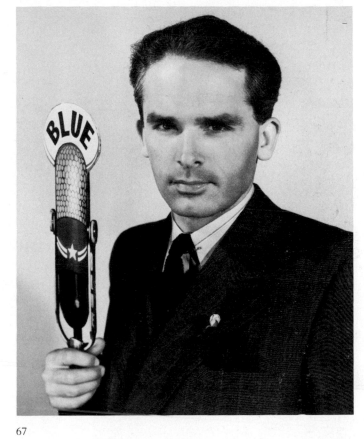

67

66. Joan Davis (1912–1961). A leading, cracked-voice comedienne of radio, television and films, Joan Davis entered show
business at the age of seven as a child comic in vaudeville. She
came to radio with Rudy Vallee in the summer of 1941, and
between 1943 and 1945 was the star of NBC's *The Sealtest Village
Store*. Miss Davis' other radio series include *Jeanie's Tea Room*
(1945–1947) and *Leave It to Joan* (1949), both CBS. Joan Davis
climbed to even greater heights of popularity on television with
her *I Married Joan* series on NBC from 1952 through 1955. Between 1942 and 1946, the comedienne was voted Queen of Comedy by the Radio Editors of America.

67. Dresser Dahlstead (1910–   ). Dahlstead entered
broadcasting as an announcer in Ogden, Utah, in 1930; he came
to NBC in San Francisco in 1932, and in 1938 transferred to NBC
in Hollywood. Named chief announcer for the Western Division
of the NBC-Blue network in 1942, Dresser Dahlstead continued
with the Blue network when it became ABC, and in 1951 was
appointed program director of the ABC Western Division. In
1959, Dahlstead left ABC to join Ralph Edwards Productions,
with which he has remained to the present. Among the best-
known programs with which Dresser Dahlstead was associated
are *Death Valley Days, I Love a Mystery* and *The Standard Symphony Hour*.

68

69

68. Dennis Day (1917–   ). Dennis Day was the resident comedy tenor on the Jack Benny program from 1939 until the show's demise. In addition, Day had his own program, *A Day in the Life of Dennis Day* (NBC, 1946–1951), and was also featured in a number of Fifties films. **69. Vaughn De Leath** (1896–1943). Vaughn De Leath was the first First Lady of Radio and the medium's first crooner, whose voice was selected by Dr. Lee De Forest as that best suited to the radio microphone. She first broadcast in January of 1920 from De Forest's experimental studio and from that moment on was always associated with radio either as a performer or executive. In the Thirties, Miss De Leath was heard at breakfast time on WMCA in New York (1934) and on her own show, on WMCA, sponsored by Lydia Pinkham (1939), as well as being a regular guest on *The Firestone Hour*. **70. Walter Damrosch** (1862–1950). Damrosch was one of the major figures in American serious music, staging the first event at Carnegie Hall in 1891, managing the Metropolitan Opera Company from 1885 to 1891, and reorganizing the New York Symphony in 1903 and remaining its director until it was merged with the New York Philharmonic in 1927. He first conducted a symphony concert on radio in 1925, and is best remembered for *The Music Appreciation Hour* on NBC-Blue from 1929 through 1942. After 20 years on the job, Damrosch retired as NBC's musical counsel in March of 1946. **71.** Minerva Pious, Kenny Delmar and Peter Donald greet Edgar Bergen and Charlie McCarthy on a special radio salute to Fred Allen, broadcast on NBC on November 14, 1965. **Kenny Delmar** (circa 1911–   ). In 1946, Kenny Delmar became the biggest star of Allen's Alley on *The Fred Allen Show* with his characterization of Senator Beauregard Claghorn, a bumptious, unreconstructed Southerner. Delmar had been active on radio since the Thirties, appearing in *The Mercury Theatre on the Air, The March of Time* and *The Shadow,* and also acting as Fred Allen's announcer. He was featured on *Your Hit Parade* (NBC, 1943) and *The Henry Morgan Show* (NBC, 1949–1950), and, as Senator Claghorn, was featured on records and in films. **Peter Donald** (1918–1979). Peter Donald, the British-born actor and dialect specialist, portrayed Ajax Cassidy, one of the residents of Allen's Alley on *The Fred Allen Show* in the Forties. Donald was also a member of the panel on *Can You Top This?* (1940–1953) and had his own 15-minute show in 1947, sponsored by Stanback Headache Powders. **Minerva Pious** (1904–1979). Russian-born Minerva Pious came to the United States at the age of two, and worked both on the stage and in films; in 1936 she replaced Fannie Brice in *The Ziegfeld Follies*. On *The Fred Allen Show,* Minerva Pious' Mrs. Nussbaum was a beloved resident of Allen's Alley, and Miss Pious was also featured on many other radio programs of the Thirties and Forties. (For Bergen and McCarthy, see No. 32.)

70

72

73

72. Cecil B. DeMille (1881–1959). One of Hollywood's great pioneering producer-directors, Cecil B. DeMille hosted *The Lux Radio Theatre* on CBS from June 1, 1936, through January 22, 1945. He might have continued for another ten years as host had he not refused to pay a one-dollar levy by the American Federation of Radio Artists needed to fight a political battle. In refusing to pay that one dollar, DeMille gave up his $100,000-a-year salary and was never again to be featured on radio. **73. Morton Downey** (1902–   ). Morton Downey began his professional career as a singer in the early Twenties, and made his radio debut in England, on the BBC, in the late Twenties. Shortly thereafter he was signed by CBS, becoming the Camel Minstrel Boy in 1931. On February 18, 1931, *Variety* described Downey as the most popular new voice on radio, and his high-pitched tenor seemed a natural for the medium. "Carolina Moon" became the singer's theme tune in the summer of 1931, replacing "Wabash Moon." Downey was almost continually on radio in the Thirties and Forties, and as late as July 15, 1949, he was the star of *The Ballad of James Otis,* a special CBS presentation in association with the American Legion Auxiliary.

74

74. Paul Douglas (1907–1959). An ex-professional football player, Paul Douglas made his radio debut on WCAU-Philadelphia and soon became a key announcer on CBS in the Thirties, working with Burns and Allen, Jack Benny, Fred Waring and the Aces, among others, and in 1937/1938 he was presenting sports talks on NBC. Douglas got his big break in 1946, when he co-starred in the Broadway hit *Born Yesterday,* and two years later he embarked on a Hollywood film career. **75. Florence Desmond** (1905–   ). The British stage and screen actress and impersonator Florence Desmond—seen here in the guise of Marlene Dietrich—had a brief vogue on American radio in 1933 after being introduced by Rudy Vallee on his Fleischmann program. Her imitations of film stars such as ZaSu Pitts, Garbo, Mae West and Tallulah Bankhead were superb.

75

76

76. Eddie Duchin (1909–1951). Pianist-bandleader Eddie Duchin was the darling of New York socialites. In between personal appearances before the smart set Duchin found time to combine melody and rhythm under the Pepsodent sponsorship on Tuesday, Thursday and Saturday nights on WJZ in New York. He was also heard on other programs such as *The Fire Chief* (NBC, 1935) and *The Victory Parade of Spotlight Bands* (Mutual, 1941). Duchin's life story was filmed in 1956. **77. Jessica Dragonette** (circa 1910–1980). To Jessica Dragonette must go the credit for popularizing operetta and semiclassical music on radio. In the Thirties, she was one of broadcasting's most popular stars, her soprano voice being heard in adaptations of many of the great operettas of the day, and in 1935 she was voted Radio's Favorite Woman Star. Miss Dragonette was first heard on radio in 1926, and her best-known series were *The Philco Hour* (NBC, 1927–1930), *Cities Service Concert* (NBC, 1929–1937), *The Palmolive Beauty Box Theatre* (CBS, 1937) and *Saturday Night Serenade* (ABC, 1944–1948). She was decorated by Pope Pius XII, made an honorary colonel in the air force in recognition of her war work, and in 1967 published her autobiography, *Faith Is a Song*. (See also Introduction figure.)

Ray Lee Jackson
N.Y.

82. Alice Faye (1915–   ) and **Phil Harris** (1904–   ). Alice Faye made her radio debut with Rudy Vallee in 1934 and that led to her extensive film career from 1934 through 1945, while Phil Harris had started broadcasting with Jack Benny in 1936. Faye and Harris were married on May 12, 1941, and beginning on September 29, 1946, starred together on *The Fitch Bandwagon*. In 1948, this program became *The Phil Harris-Alice Faye Show* and it continued on radio as NBC's answer to *Amos 'n' Andy* (heard the same time on Sunday evenings) through 1954. **83. Clifton Fadiman** (1904–   ). A distinguished man of letters, Clifton Fadiman moderated the popular quiz *Information Please* from 1938 through 1948, and later hosted *Conversation* from 1954 through 1957. **84. Jinx Falkenburg** (1919–   ). One-time cover girl, occasional film actress and *Life* magazine's number-one girl for 1941, Jinx Falkenburg, with her husband Tex McCrary, hosted the most popular breakfast show of the Forties, *Hi, Jinx!*, originating out of WEAF-New York in 1946 and continuing well into the Fifties. Later the two were to be heard on NBC on an evening program, *Tex and Jinx,* describing themselves as "the first husband-and-wife breakfast team to stay on the air for dinner." During the 12 years that the McCrarys were on radio and television, they interviewed over 16,000 guests.

82

83

84

85. Jimmy Fidler (1900–   ). Fidler began his newspaper career in the early Twenties, after appearing in a few silent films. He made his radio debut in 1932, and quickly gained a reputation for the crisp and caustic comments he had to offer on Hollywood personalities and films. A typical introduction would be, "This is Jimmy Fidler from Hollywood, where they marry for better or worse, but not for long." His remarks got him into a lot of trouble with the studios and he was frequently regarded as persona non grata, but nonetheless his network radio programs continued through the early Fifties, and he still broadcasts today on several local stations.   **86. Gracie Fields** (1898–1979). The popular British music-hall and film star made her U.S. radio debut on Campbell's *Hollywood Hotel* on CBS on April 30, 1937, and *Variety* thought she sounded like Polly Moran with a voice. Nevertheless, Gracie Fields was back in 1942 with her own nightly five-minute program for NBC-Blue, sponsored by Pall Mall; in 1943 the show expanded to 15 minutes on the Mutual network, and by 1944 ran a full 30 minutes. In addition, Gracie Fields was a featured guest star on many other radio shows and during 1951 and 1952 she was heard on her own show, again for Mutual. *Variety* (October 20, 1943) had to admit, "The Lancashire singer-comedienne is a great entertainer, whose vitality and irresistible personality overcome her frankly inadequate voice."   **87. Elsie Ferguson** (1885–1961). A beautiful and adroit stage actress who also had a major film career from 1917 through 1922, Elsie Ferguson made her radio debut on *Ward's Family Theatre,* over the CBS network, on Sunday, May 13, 1934. She was heard in subsequent weeks on that program recreating some of her major stage roles. During 1935 and 1936, Elsie Ferguson could be heard on a 15-minute political program, *The Crusaders,* in which she addressed herself to the women of the nation on the evils of political dictatorship and the New Deal.

85

86

87

89

88

88. W. C. Fields (1880–1946). A major star of vaudeville, *Ziegfeld Follies* and films, W. C. Fields made his first radio appearance on a regular series on May 9, 1937, when his famous inflammatory confrontations with Charlie McCarthy began; they continued on a semi-regular basis from 1941 through 1944. In addition, Fields was a regular in 1938 on NBC's *Your Hit Parade*. **89. Ted Fio Rito** (1900–1971). A famous composer-bandleader of the Twenties, Thirties and Forties, Ted Fio Rito composed many popular songs, including "Laugh, Clown, Laugh," and gave work with his orchestra to many celebrities-to-be, some of whom were Betty Grable, Lucille Ball, June Haver and David Rose. Among the many radio programs on which Ted Fio Rito was featured are *Presenting Al Jolson* (NBC, 1932), *Hollywood Hotel* (CBS, 1934–1937) and *The Jack Haley Show* (NBC and CBS, 1937–1939).

90

90. Alice Frost (birth year unavailable). Alice Frost made her radio debut on WMCA in the mid-Thirties, after extensive stage work; she was the star of *Big Sister* (CBS, 1936–1942), *Les Misérables* (Mutual, 1937), *Woman of Courage* (CBS, 1940–1942) and, of course, *Mr. and Mrs. North* (NBC and CBS, 1942–1952). She worked with Orson Welles on the stage and in *The Mercury Theatre on the Air,* and also worked with Al Pearce, Stoopnagle and Budd, Jimmy Durante (in *Jumbo*), Robert Benchley and Robert Ripley, and was also to be heard on *News Parade, The Clock* and *The Second Mrs. Burton.* Miss Frost was described in 1939 as the Busiest Actress on Broadway, has worked extensively in television—she was Aunt Trina in *Mama*—and is still active today. She is seen in the photo with Joseph Curtin (as Mr. and Mrs. North). **91. Jane Froman** (1908–1980). Today, Jane Froman is best remembered for her struggle back to stardom after a near-fatal plane crash in 1943, a struggle recorded in the 1952 film *With a Song in My Heart,* starring Susan Hayward. A strong personality with a rich contralto voice, Miss Froman came to fame on WENR-Chicago in 1931 after earlier broadcasts on WLS-Cincinnati. Among her many radio programs were *The Intimate Revue* (NBC-Blue, 1934–1935), *The Gulf Oil Show* (CBS, 1939) and *The Pause That Refreshes* (CBS, 1948). **92. Arlene Francis** (1908–   ). A stage and screen actress who will always be remembered for the years she spent on television's *What's My Line?,* Arlene Francis was a busy actress and all-round personality on radio from the Thirties onward. Aside from brief periods on *Betty and Bob* (NBC) and *The Hour of Charm* (CBS), Miss Francis was a regular on *What's My Name?* (Mutual, NBC and ABC, 1938–1949), *Blind Date* (NBC, 1943–1945) and *The Affairs of Ann Scotland* (ABC, 1946–1947).

91

92

93

94

93. The Funnyboners. The Funnyboners were a comedy singing trio consisting of Gordon Graham (smiling in the photo) David Grant (with the microphone) and Bunny Coughlin, who would begin their act singing, "We are the funnyboners and we hope you won't disown us." Very popular on early radio, by 1932 the Funnyboners were to be heard three times a week on CBS. **94. Jan Garber** (circa 1895–1977). A popular orchestra leader on radio in the Thirties and Forties, Jan Garber formed his first band at the age of 21 with pianist Milton Davis, together with whom he composed his theme song, "My Dear." Garber was noted for the sweet sound of his music, although he did try swing in the early Forties. **95. Ed Gardner** (1901–1963). Ed Gardner had been a radio director (he worked for a while with Rudy Vallee) before creating the character of Archie of *Duffy's Tavern*, initially on a 1939 CBS program, *This Is New York*. *Duffy's Tavern* became a popular favorite on CBS in 1941 and was heard through 1951, later moving over to NBC. Ed Gardner's Archie was the master of the wrong word in the right place, while Gardner's real wife (from 1929 to 1942) Shirley Booth

played Miss Duffy. **96. Betty Garde** (1905–   ). Stage and screen actress Betty Garde, who made her professional debut in 1922 and is best known as Aunt Eller in the original production of *Oklahoma!*, was very active on radio from the Thirties through the Fifties. Among the programs on which Miss Garde was heard are *Les Misérables* (Mutual, 1937), *Lorenzo Jones* (NBC, 1937–1955), *My Son and I* (CBS, 1939–1940), *Policewoman* (ABC, 1946), *The Fat Man* (ABC, 1946–1951) and *The Big Story* (NBC, 1947–1955). She worked with Eddie Cantor, Kate Smith, Milton Berle and Goodman Ace, played every wanted woman on *Gang Busters* and was Madame X for Ex-Lax. **97. George Gershwin** (1898–1937). The composer of some of the best popular music of the twentieth century (including *Rhapsody in Blue* and *An American in Paris*) and the scores for some of the century's best-known shows (*Porgy and Bess; Lady, Be Good!; Funny Face* and *Girl Crazy*) did not overlook radio. Gershwin had his own twice-weekly program, *Music by Gershwin*, on WJZ, sponsored by Feenamint, which was first heard on February 19, 1934. By 1935, the Gershwin program was heard only once a week.

95

96

97

98

99

98. Floyd Gibbons (1887–1939). A war correspondent turned radio commentator whose eyepatch—he had lost an eye during the First World War—gave him an air of drama and mystery, Floyd Gibbons was heard regularly between 1932 and 1936 under the sponsorship of Colgate-Palmolive, Armour, RCA and others. He was noted for his on-the-spot broadcasts and for his rapid-fire style of announcing. With Lowell Thomas, Gibbons had been responsible for *Headline Hunters,* one of NBC's earliest news broadcasts, first heard in 1929. **99.** Arthur Godfrey (right) gives Herb Shriner some pointers on *Arthur Godfrey's Talent Scouts,* which the latter was to emcee while Godfrey was on vacation during the summer of 1951. **Arthur Godfrey** (1903–   ). Arthur Godfrey has been described as "radio's one-man show," an entertainer who could entertain by simply chatting with his audience. Godfrey entered radio in 1930 with WFBR in Baltimore, and the same year joined NBC as an announcer. He moved to CBS in 1934, remaining with that network for almost 40 years, although he did find time to work elsewhere, such as Mutual with a 15-minute show for Barbasol during 1937 and 1938. It was in the Forties that Godfrey came to the fore in radio, noted for his criticism of the advertisers' products and for programs such as *Victory Begins at Home* (1942), produced to boost civilian morale, *Arthur Godfrey's Talent Scouts,* beginning in 1942, *Arthur Godfrey Time,* beginning in 1945, and *Arthur Godfrey's Digest,* beginning in 1952. He presented his farewell radio show on April 30, 1972. **Herb Shriner** (1918–1970). Herb Shriner, the Hoosier Humorist, entered radio at the age of 17, and by 1942 was the star of *The Camel Caravan.* He had his own program, *Herb Shri-*

ner Time, on CBS from 1948 through 1949, and in 1951 was a summer replacement for Arthur Godfrey on both radio and television. This stint led to an extensive career in the latter medium. **100. Bert Gordon** (1895–1974). Bert Gordon was the Mad Russian of radio and films, noted for his dialect greeting of "How do you do?" He was a regular on Eddie Cantor's program from 1935 through 1949. **101. Benny Goodman** (1909–   ). The King of Swing, Benny Goodman began his professional career as a clarinetist with Bix Beiderbecke. He formed his own dance band in 1934 and that same year was signed by NBC. Benny Goodman and radio were as synonymous as Benny Goodman and swing in the Thirties and Forties. **102. Richard Gordon** (1882–?). Aside from Basil Rathbone, Richard Gordon was radio's Sherlock Holmes for the longest period of time, from 1931 through 1935 on NBC, under the sponsorship of George Washington Coffee. Gordon was also to be heard on many soap operas and other programs through the Forties, including *The Bishop and the Gargoyle, Follow the Moon, Jane Arden, Orphans of Divorce, Pepper Young's Family, Stella Dallas* and *Valiant Lady.* **103. Gale Gordon** (1906–   ). Before he became Lucille Ball's best-known male sidekick, Gale Gordon had been active in radio from the early Thirties. Among the many programs on which he appeared are *Big Town; The Shadow of Fu Manchu* (from the Thirties); *The Casebook of Gregory Hood; The Great Gildersleeve; Johnny Madero, Pier 23; Junior Miss* and *My Favorite Husband* (from the Forties). He will always be remembered for his eight years with *Fibber McGee and Molly* as the Old Timer, etc., and as Osgood Conklin on *Our Miss Brooks.*

100

101

102

103

104

104. Tito Guizar (1912–   ). With his pleasant tenor voice, bright smile and guitar, Tito Guizar was a welcome performer on radio from 1932 onward. In addition to radio, Guizar was featured in films and still remains active, now making his home in his native Mexico.

105

106

107

105. Ben Grauer (1908–1977). Benjamin Franklin Grauer joined NBC in 1930 and quickly became its senior commentator and reporter. He was announcer for Henry Morgan, Walter Winchell, *Information Please* (in the Forties) and the NBC Symphony Orchestra (1940–1954). Grauer covered every major historic event, including the Morro Castle Fire, the Paris Peace Conference and the U.S. occupation of Japan. Eleven times between 1951 and 1969, Grauer covered the New Year's Eve celebrations in Times Square for both radio and television. He provided the commentary for NBC's first television special, the opening of the New York World's Fair in 1939, and, with John Cameron Swayze, presented the first live television coverage of the national political conventions in 1948. Aside from his work as an announcer and commentator, Grauer found time to host such shows as *Pot o' Gold* (1939–1941). **106. Johnny Green** (1908–   ). Johnny Green, who now calls himself John Green, is a major figure in American popular music, a noted composer, conductor and arranger who was extremely busy on radio in the Thirties, working with Ruth Etting, Jack Benny, Fred Astaire and others. Green later went to Hollywood, where he has won five Academy Awards and has been nominated for nine more. **107. Jack Haley** (1899–1979). Jack Haley was already a star of vaudeville, musical comedy and films when he began his first radio series on NBC in 1937, following his appearances on the Maxwell House *Show Boat* earlier that same year. The comedian is best known (in radio) as the host of *The Sealtest Village Store* (NBC, 1942–1947).

A127-1

109

110

108. The Happiness Boys: Billy Jones (at left in photo; 1889–1940) and Ernie Hare (1883–1939). Billy Jones and Ernie Hare were radio's Happiness Boys, two of the medium's first stars, with their theme song, "We two boys without a care entertain you folks out there. That's our hap-hap-happiness!" After working in revue, Jones and Hare entered broadcasting in 1921 and got their tag name from their first sponsor on WEAF, Happiness Candy Stores of New York. When the pair were sponsored by Interwoven Hosiery, they became known as the Interwoven Pair and were later the Flit Soldiers, under the sponsorship of Standard Oil. In 1933, the Happiness Boys had their own program on NBC-Blue and in 1936 they were featured on CBS. At the time of Hare's death, the Happiness Boys were to be heard on *The Three Little Sachs* on WMCA, and, after his partner's death, Jones continued on that program with Hare's daughter

Marilyn. *Variety* (March 15, 1939) described the Happiness Boys as "the first singing and patter act to achieve national radio fame." **109. Radie Harris** (birth year unavailable). The popular film columnist Radie Harris, whose feature "Broadway Ballyhoo" appears regularly in *The Hollywood Reporter,* has had probably the longest career on radio of any of her ilk, including Louella Parsons and Hedda Hopper. Miss Harris made her debut on WOR-New York in 1930 and has been broadcasting almost continually since. **110. Dick Haymes** (1918–1980). Dick Haymes was a popular baritone of the Forties, a close rival to Frank Sinatra. Haymes first came to the forefront with Harry James and His Orchestra in 1939. Aside from frequent guest appearances, he was to be heard on *Here's to Romance* (CBS, 1943–1945), *The Dick Haymes Show* (NBC and CBS, 1944–1947) and *I Fly Anything* (ABC, 1950–1951).

112

111

111. Gabriel Heatter (circa 1891–1972). Gabriel Heatter was a Hearst newspaperman turned radio reporter and commentator, best remembered as the host and interviewer for *We the People* on CBS in the late Thirties and early Forties, and for his Second World War broadcasts, which he would open with the words, "Ah, yes, there's good news tonight." Heatter retired from network broadcasting in 1960, and his last broadcast, on a Miami station, was on May 23, 1965. **112. Horace Heidt** (1901–   ). A showman as much as a musician, Horace Heidt first came to radio on WJZ in January of 1931. Among his early radio broadcasts were *Ship of Joy* and *Answers for Dancers* (both in 1932). Heidt's first major series was *Anniversary Night,* first heard on CBS on February 2, 1935, which ran through 1937. At that time, it was Horace Heidt and His Brigadiers, but in 1939 the band became Horace Heidt and His Musical Knights. Heidt's best known programs were *Pot 'o Gold* (NBC, 1939–1941) and *Youth Opportunity Program* (NBC and CBS, 1947–1953). In 1955 Heidt retired and now concentrates on his real-estate interests.

113

114

113. Jean Hersholt (1886–1956). Jean Hersholt, who had a long and distinguished career as a character actor in both silent and sound films, first played Dr. Christian in the 1936 film *The Country Doctor*. This feature led to a series of six films for RKO between 1939 and 1941 and the radio series, on CBS, from 1937 through 1953. In addition to his acting, Hersholt was prominent in film-industry and charitable activities and President of the Academy of Motion Picture Arts and Sciences between 1947 and 1949. **114. Hildegarde** (1906–   ). Hildegarde Sell of Milwaukee, Wisconsin, made her first major radio appearance on *The Fleischmann Hour* on July 30, 1936, singing "These Foolish Things Remind Me of You" and "Life Story of a Piano." Within a couple of years she had become the incomparable Hildegarde, earning $150,000 a year, whose theme song "Darling, Je Vous Aime Beaucoup" will always be associated with her. Hildegarde was to be heard on *Ninety Men and a Girl* (CBS, 1939) and *Beat the Band* (NBC, 1943), among other shows. *Life* (November 1, 1943) described her as "An effective song salesman with a husk in her voice."

121

122

123

124

121. Leon Janney (1917–1980). *The Saturday Evening Post* (February 19, 1949) described Janney as "one of the most successful of the 2,000-odd free lance actors who earn their living exclusively from radio." In a typical year, 1949, he could be heard as Charlie Chan's number-one son on Mutual every Monday, as Captain Arthur Duncan in *Backstage Wife* on NBC Monday through Friday and as Jerry Feldman in *Pepper Young's Family,* also on NBC Monday through Friday. Janney had a remarkable career which began when he was two and embraced stage, screen, radio and television. As late as 1960 he was to be heard on *The Romance of Helen Trent* on CBS. **122. Al Jolson** (1886–1950). Al Jolson was one of this century's greatest entertainers, equally at home on stage, screen and radio. He was first heard on the last in 1927, but only came into his own in the Thirties, starring in *The Al Jolson Show* (1932–1933), *The Kraft Music Hall* (1933–1934) and *Shell Chateau* (1935–1936), all on NBC, and in *The Lifebuoy Program* (1936–1939) on CBS. Up until the day of his death, Jolson was a welcome guest on the most popular radio programs of the time, and, in addition, starred in seven *Lux Radio Theatre* shows from *Burlesque* in 1936 through *Jolson Sings Again* in 1950. Jolson was last heard, broadcasting from Korea on CBS for Louella Parsons, on September 15, 1950; death prevented his guest appearance on the October 24, 1950, *Bing Crosby Show.* **123. Spike Jones** (1911–1965). Spike Jones, the musical satirist who became a national institution with his recordings of "Chloe," "Cocktails for Two" and his first big hit, "Der Fuehrer's Face," was a popular guest star of Forties radio programs and had his own show on CBS from 1947 through 1949. As Jones once remarked of his raucous music, which featured everything from cowbells to dog barks, "We were too corny for sophisticated people and too sophisticated for corny people." **124. Jim** (1896–   ) and **Marian** (1897–1961) **Jordan.** Jim and Marian Jordon were Fibber McGee and Molly, the leading citizens of 79 Wistful Vista, Peoria, who, thanks to their radio audience, "gave Peoria its 28,000,000 population." Marian Driscoll and Jim Jordan were married on August 21, 1918, and first came to radio in Chicago in 1924. *Fibber McGee and Molly* was first heard on the NBC-Blue Network on April 16, 1935, and continued a radio favorite through 1957. Of the first program, *Variety* (April 24, 1935) had written, "more a slipshod musical hour than a refreshing down-to-earth comedy serial," but by 1944 the program was carried by 133 NBC stations and affiliates. To most radio listeners, *Fibber McGee and Molly* brings back memories of Molly's put-down, "T'ain't funny, McGee," and McGee's infamous, crowded closet.

125

126

127

125. H. V. Kaltenborn (1878–1965). Known as the dean of radio news commentators, Hans Von Kaltenborn graduated from *The Brooklyn Daily Eagle* to radio commentating in 1922, but it was not until 1929 that he joined CBS to become its chief news analyst through 1940, when he moved to NBC. As Robert Landry wrote in *Variety* (June 16, 1965), "He had a splendor of voice trained by decades on the lecture platform, and an authoritative editorial writing manner which the anxieties and confusions of the epoch greatly welcomed." **126. Ish Kabibble** (1908–   ). Ish Kabibble was, in reality, Merwyn A. Bogue, a trumpeter turned comedian with Kay Kyser. He wore his hair in what has come to be known as a Beatles cut and sang novelty songs such as "Don't Drop a Slug in a Slot" and "Three Little Fishes" on *Kay Kyser's Kollege of Musical Knowledge*. (See also Introduction figure.) **127. Danny Kaye** (1913–   ). Vaudeville comic Danny Kaye was hailed as a star as a result of his appearance in the 1940 Broadway hit *Lady in the Dark*. In 1944, he commenced his feature-film career with Samuel Goldwyn and the following year began his own show on CBS. (He had appeared very occasionally on local radio in the Thirties.) On the stage, Kaye was regarded as much as a pantomime artist as a vocal comic, and *Time* (January 15, 1945) was pleased to note, "He proved he could be funny in the dark."

128

129

128. **William Keighley** (1889–   ). The Broadway actor-turned-film-director (1932–1953) William Keighley was the eventual permanent choice to replace Cecil B. DeMille on *The Lux Radio Theatre*. He was first heard on the program as the permanent host on November 5, 1945, and remained with the series through 1954. 129. **Dorothy Kirsten** (1917–   ). A blonde lyric soprano, equally at home in opera and semiclassical music, Dorothy Kirsten made her operatic debut with the Chicago Civic Opera Company on November 9, 1940. Prior to that, she had begun her career as a radio singer on WINS-New York in 1938, and then had become a protégée of Grace Moore. On radio, Miss Kirsten is best remembered for *Keepsakes* (NBC-Blue, 1943–1944), *The Kraft Music Hall* (NBC, 1947–1949) and *Light Up Time* (NBC, 1949). 130. **Kay Kyser** (1906–   ). With his familiar greeting of "Evenin', folks! How y'all?" Kay Kyser was a popular radio staple from the mid-Thirties onward, best known for *Kay Kyser's Kollege of Musical Knowledge,* heard from 1938 through 1949. Harry Babbitt and Ginny Simms were the featured singers on the show and the theme song was "Thinking of You." Kyser had organized his first orchestra while a student at the University of North Carolina in 1926; he retired in 1951. (See also Introduction figure.)

130

131

132

131. André Kostelanetz (1901–1980). André Kostelanetz was noted for his easy-to-take versions of the classics. Born in Russia, he came to the United States in 1922, and six years later joined CBS as an arranger and conductor. It is claimed that Kostelanetz was the first to mix classical and popular music on radio, which he did on June 1, 1932, on a program that included "Alabamy Bound" and the third movement of Tchaikovsky's Fourth Symphony. A busy conductor on radio in the Thirties and Forties, in 1952 Kostelanetz became guest conductor of the New York Philharmonic, a position that he held until his death. **132. Arthur Lake** (1905–   ) and **Penny Singleton** (1909–   ). Both Lake and Singleton were long-time film performers before commencing the *Blondie* series for Columbia, in which they played Dagwood Bumstead and Blondie, respectively. Twenty-eight *Blondie* films were produced between 1938 and 1950, and from 1939 through 1948 Lake and Singleton starred in the radio version of the comic strip on NBC. Penny Singleton was replaced on the radio show in 1949 by Patricia Van Cleve, and one year later embarked on her own radio show on NBC. Lake stayed with the Dagwood Bumstead character longer, playing the role also in a popular Fifties television series. **133. Frances Langford** (1914–   ). Frances Langford made her radio debut on a Tampa station in 1932. It was Rudy Vallee who brought her to network radio, and she was a frequent guest singer on variety shows as well as a regular on *The Bob Hope Show* in the late Thirties. With Don Ameche, Miss Langford created the comedy routine of *The Bickersons* on *The Charlie McCarthy Show,* and the two took *The Bickersons* to NBC in 1946 and CBS in 1947. Later, Langford teamed with Lew Parker to perform as *The Bickersons* on CBS in 1951. Her extensive film career, which began in 1935, did not equal the stature of her radio work.

134. Jesse L. Lasky (1880–1958). Lasky was a pioneering Hollywood producer, who co-founded Paramount Pictures in the early Teens and remained active in the film industry until his death. The producer devised and introduced a 30-minute amateur talent contest which offered winners contracts with RKO and was first heard on CBS on Sunday, January 8, 1939; the only major personality to be discovered on Lasky's program was Gale Storm. When Cecil B. DeMille quit *The Lux Radio Theatre,* it was his wish that Lasky replace him, but that was not to be. **135. Pinky Lee** (1916–   ). The lisping burlesque comic with the funny hat had been active on radio since the Thirties, featured on such programs as *Carefree Carnival* (NBC, mid-Thirties), *Drene Time* (NBC, late Forties) and *Tonight at Hoagy's* (CBS, mid-Forties). Pinky Lee is best remembered, of course, as the star of one of the most popular children's television shows of the Fifties. **136. Oscar Levant** (1906–1972). Oscar Levant, a brilliant, witty and neurotic concert pianist and composer, was once described by Henry Morgan as "possibly the world's oldest living brat." Radio listeners enjoyed Levant on NBC's *Information Please* from 1938 through 1943, but Levant himself noted, "My appeal is to a select few and they are in danger of being arrested."

134

135

136

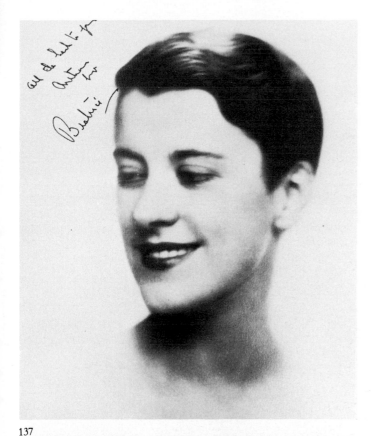

137. Beatrice Lillie (circa 1894–   ). Beatrice Lillie, a multi-talented singer, actress and comedienne, first seen on the stage in the mid-Teens, was much in demand as a guest star on radio variety shows in the Thirties and Forties; the parody of *Oklahoma!* with Fred Allen is fondly remembered. Beginning in January of 1935, Miss Lillie had her own program on NBC, sponsored by Borden, but the network was so concerned that its star might prove too sophisticated for American audiences that it went to the trouble of sending out a special news release, explaining: "Through her inimitable characterizations and laugh-provoking songs, with their special lyrics and intentionally off-pitch tones she will poke fun at silly vanities and practices." **138. Guy Lombardo** (1902–1977). In 1927 Guy Lombardo changed the name of his orchestra to the Royal Canadians, and that same year he made his radio debut on WBBM-Chicago. Two years later, Lombardo began broadcasting over the CBS network, and on December 31, 1929, he inaugurated his New Year's Eve network radio show. It was indeed "the sweetest music this side of Heaven." **139. Art Linkletter** (1912–   ). Art Linkletter began his radio career in 1933 as an announcer for KGB-San Diego, and by the mid-Forties was the medium's foremost master of ceremonies. From shows such as *What's Doin' Ladies?* (NBC, 1943–1945) he graduated to *People Are Funny* (NBC and CBS, 1943–1959). Linkletter's best-known radio program was *House Party,* which made its debut on CBS on January 15, 1945, and ran through October 13, 1967; a television version was first seen on September 1, 1952.

137

138

139

140

141

140. Nick Lucas (1897–   ). The gentle singing voice of Nick Lucas was first heard on radio in the Twenties when Lucas was working for Ted Fio Rito at the Edgewater Beach Hotel in Chicago. After recording "Tip Toe Thru the Tulips with Me" in 1929, Lucas' popularity was assured, and he became a regular on radio in the Thirties, being placed under contract to CBS in 1934. **141. Vincent Lopez** (1894–1975). With his theme song, "Nola," and his introduction, "Lopez speaking," Vincent Lopez became a national figure on radio. Lopez was the first conductor to lead his orchestra live from WJZ in 1921 and the first bandleader to be heard by remote pickup on radio, while playing at New York's Pennsylvania Grill in 1921. Calvin Coolidge supposedly told the conductor, "I like the way you introduce numbers. You just give the name of the song, then play it. Most announcers talk too much." Vincent Lopez continued to be heard on radio through the Fifties and was also a regular on television.

142

143

142. Lum and Abner: Chester Lauck (1902–1980; left) and Norris Goff (1906–1978). Lauck was Lum Edwards and Goff was Abner Peabody in *Lum and Abner,* a comedy series best described as a white *Amos 'n' Andy*. Lauck and Goff were first heard on KTHA-Hot Springs, Arkansas, on April 26, 1931, and later that year came to the NBC network and remained on network radio through 1953. Lum and Abner were the proprietors of the Jot Em Down Store in Pine Ridge, Arkansas, and so popular was the program that in 1936 the township of Waters, Arkansas, changed its name to Pine Ridge. In addition to radio, the Lum and Abner characters were featured in half-a-dozen feature films and a couple of shorts. **143. Abe Lyman** (1897–1957). The veteran bandleader and composer ("I Cried for You," etc.) began his career in Chicago in 1916. Lyman began to be heard on KMTR in Los Angeles after many years as the resident orchestra leader at the Carthay Circle Theatre and the Roosevelt Hotel in that city. On network radio, Lyman could be heard on such programs as *Waltz Time* (NBC, 1933) and, in 1935, was voted twelfth in popularity among radio's bandleaders.

144

145

144. Knox Manning (1904–1980). The career of this popular radio announcer, who began on KNW-Los Angeles in the early Thirties, came to a virtual end after the Second World War following a throat operation. He was president of the American Federation of Radio Artists, 1950–1952, and the first chairman of the American Federation of Radio and Television Artists in 1952. **145. Gordon MacRae** (1921–   ). An appealing baritone who will always be associated with the film roles of Curly in *Oklahoma!* (1955) and Billy Bigelow in *Carousel* (1956), Gordon MacRae first came to radio with Horace Heidt in 1940. After two years with Heidt, MacRae branched out on his own. He had a 15-minute spot, Tuesdays and Thursdays, on NBC for Gulf Oil in 1947, and starred on *Texaco Star Theatre* (CBS, 1947, and ABC, 1948), but is best remembered for *The Railroad Hour* (NBC, 1949–1954). *Life* (July 5, 1949) described MacRae as "radio's most versatile singer."

146

147

146. Freddy Martin (1907–   ). A big name in big bands, Freddy Martin was the resident orchestra leader at Los Angeles' Cocoanut Grove for 25 years, beginning there on December 17, 1940. Describing his music as "upper middle of the road," Martin had his own show on CBS in 1941, for Lady Esther, and also played for *The Jack Carson Show,* first heard on CBS in 1943. **147. Johnny Marvin** (1897–1944). A popular radio singer of the Thirties—he had his own show on NBC for five years—Johnny Marvin was billed as the Lonesome Singer of the Air. This melodious, though untrained, tenor was also a composer, writing the songs for many of the Gene Autry westerns. **148. Groucho Marx** (1890–1977).   The best-known of the Marx Brothers, Groucho was also the best-equipped for a radio career and was a frequent guest star from the early Thirties. Marx had a number of series on radio, including *The Circle* (NBC, 1939), *Blue Ribbon Town* (CBS, 1943–1944) and, of course, *You Bet Your Life,* heard on all three networks at one time or another between 1947 and 1959.

148

149

149. Mary Margaret McBride (1899–1976). Newspaperwoman and magazine writer Mary Margaret McBride was the undisputed first lady of radio. Her talk show was first heard over the CBS network in 1937, moved to NBC in 1941 and finished up on ABC in 1950. She was noted for making her guests feel comfortable "by telling a story about them that's funny or sweet." Miss McBride made her radio debut on WOR-New York in 1934; she celebrated her tenth anniversary on the air with a party at Madison Square Garden, opened by Mrs. Roosevelt, and her fifteenth anniversary with a shindig at Yankee Stadium, attended by 50,000 and including a speech titled "Mary Margaret McBride I Love You" by Eva Le Gallienne. Mary Margaret McBride retired from network radio in 1954 to try her hand at television, but was still conducting a local radio show from her living room in the Catskills at the time of her death.

150

150. Don McNeill (1907–   ). Don McNeill hosted the longest-running morning program on radio, *The Breakfast Club*, heard for one hour, Mondays through Fridays, from 1933 through 1968. The program was a mixture of music, jokes—all totally unsophisticated—and what one magazine described as "well-planned spontaneity." He is seen here with two former Earl Carroll girls. **151. Graham McNamee** (1888–1942). After making his debut as a baritone at Aeolian Hall, New York, in 1920, Graham McNamee joined WEAF in 1923. He was one of NBC's best-loved reporters and announcers, remaining with the network until his death 19 years later.

151

152

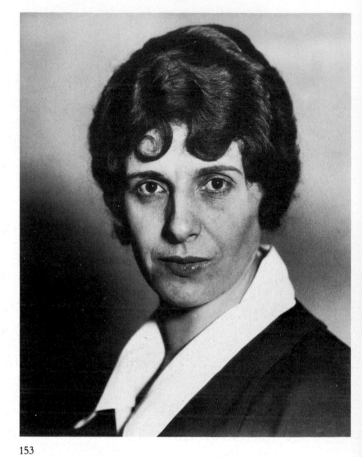

153

152. Burgess Meredith (1908–   ). Burgess Meredith began his professional career as a member of Eva Le Gallienne's Student Repertory Group in the late Twenties; his first major stage success came in 1935 with *Winterset,* the film version of which marked Meredith's screen debut the following year. The actor's radio debut was as Red Adams (later Red Davis) in the soap opera of that name, first heard on the NBC-Blue network on October 2, 1932, and later to become (without Meredith) *Pepper Young's Family*. Meredith was a memorable Hamlet on CBS, July 9, 1937, with Grace George; other one-shot radio appearances include *Birth of a Nation* (CBS, 1940), *People with Light Coming Out of Them* (CBS, 1941) and The Theatre Guild on the Air presenta- tions of *Wings Over Europe* (CBS, 1945) and *The Taming of the Shrew* (CBS, 1937). In addition, Meredith was master of cere- monies on *The Pursuit of Happiness* (CBS, 1939) and *We the People* (CBS, 1941). **153. Aimee Semple McPherson** (1890–1944). The radio broadcasts of the evangelist and founder of the Inter- national Church of the Foursquare Gospel were, in every sense of the word, shows. Aimee would use modern slang and when she muffed a Bible quotation would wind up with "and so on ...." The evangelist always began her broadcasts with the words, "You thousands of people here, you in the orchestra, you in the first balcony, you in the second balcony, you crowds standing in the rear, you thousands listening in over the radio."

154

154. The Mills Brothers (left to right: Herbert, Harry, Donald). The Mills Brothers originally consisted of Herbert, Harry, Donald and John; when John died in 1936 he was replaced by John Mills, Sr., and when *he* retired in 1957 the group became a trio. The brothers were first heard on radio on WLW–Cincinnati in 1925, and by 1932 were regarded as some of the biggest moneymakers on radio, heard over the CBS network under the sponsorship of Procter & Gamble. Using their voices like musical instruments, the Mills Brothers were featured on such programs as Friday night's *Elgin Watch Hour* (1935), on which their theme song was "Time on My Hands."

155

156

157

158

155. Vaughn Monroe (1911–1973). The crooning baritone and bandleader with his self-composed theme song, "Racing with the Moon," was known as the Man with Muscles on His Tonsils. Vaughn Monroe was the Forties' answer to Rudy Vallee and had his own program on CBS from 1946 through 1954. He is seen here with the Moon Maids. **156. Molasses and January:** Pick Malone (1892–1962) and Pat Padgett (1903–   ). Blackface comedians Malone and Padgett were first heard on radio with the WOR Minstrels in 1929. They changed their billing to Molasses and January for the Maxwell House *Show Boat,* first heard on NBC on October 6, 1932, and then become Pick and Pat again on CBS. As Molasses and January they returned to radio in 1941 on *Dr. Pepper Parade* and in September of 1942 were to be heard, Mondays through Fridays, on NBC-Blue with a five-minute comedy news comment, on which they were billed as America's Advisors on the Home Front. **157. Garry Moore** (1915–   ). Garry Moore entered radio with WBAL-Baltimore in the mid-Thirties and later moved to the NBC network, working on *Club Matinee* (1939) and *Beat the Band* (1940), among others. Moore is best remembered for *The Camel Caravan* (CBS, 1943–1947),

on which he made a perfect partner to Jimmy Durante. *Take It or Leave It* (NBC, 1947–1948) and *Breakfast in Hollywood* (ABC, 1948–1949) followed, and then came *The Garry Moore Show* (CBS, 1949–1950), which led to his own television series. **158. Agnes Moorehead** (1906–1974). Agnes Moorehead probably spent more time on radio than she did on the stage and in films, with which she is usually associated. Miss Moorehead made her radio debut as a singer in St. Louis in 1923 and was featured in the Twenties series *Seth Parker.* Agnes Moorehead was Mrs. Heartburn on *The Phil Baker Show* in 1935 and *Calamity Jane* on CBS in 1946; among the other series in which she appeared are *Les Misérables* (Mutual, 1937), *The Shadow* (CBS, 1937–1939) and *Bringing Up Father* (NBC, 1941). The actress worked frequently with Orson Welles, particularly in *The Mercury Theatre on the Air,* and was the star of the first episode of *The CBS Radio Mystery Theatre* on January 6, 1974. The radio role which will always be associated with Agnes Moorehead is that of Mrs. Stevenson in *Sorry, Wrong Number,* first heard in the CBS series *Suspense* on May 25, 1947.

181

180

180. Ben Pollack (1903–1971). After Pollack's tragic suicide, critic Leonard Feather rightly described him as a "fallen giant of jazz." After working as a drummer with the New Orleans Rhythm Kings from 1922 through 1924, Pollack left to form his own band. He became a fixture at New York's Park Central Hotel, giving Benny Goodman his first major job, and was a popular favorite on radio during the Thirties and Forties. **181. Jane Pickens** (birth year unavailable). Jane Pickens, along with her sisters Patti and Helen, came to radio, on NBC, in 1931, and the girls remained together as a trio until 1936, when Jane went into the *Ziegfeld Follies* as a replacement for Gertrude Niesen. A melodic soprano, Jane Pickens was a featured soloist on radio, working with Ben Bernie and having her own show on NBC in 1948; as late as 1950, she was the star of NBC's *The Chamber Music Society of Lower Basin Street*. **182. Mary Pickford** (1893–1979). America's sweetheart turned to radio after her film career was over and, in the late Thirties and early Forties, was to be heard on two programs, *Mary Pickford and Buddy Rogers* and *Parties at Pickfair*. Later, Pickford's third husband, Buddy Rogers, tried his hand at broadcasting, minus his better half.

183

184

183. Basil Rathbone (1892–1967). The popular British stage
and screen actor, who is best known for the 15 films in which
he appeared as Sherlock Holmes between 1939 and 1946, also
appeared as the radio Sherlock Holmes during the same period,
first on NBC-Blue and later on Mutual. Rathbone was first heard
as Holmes on Monday, October 2, 1939, in "The Case of the
Sussex Vampire," sponsored by Grove Bromo-Quinine. Two
years later, *Variety* (October 8, 1941) commented, "One of radio's
most satisfying acts is that of Basil Rathbone as Sherlock
Holmes." In addition, Rathbone was heard as Inspector Burke
on the 1947 *Scotland Yard* series on Mutual. **184. Irene Rich**
(1891–   ). Irene Rich was a dignified and striking screen actress, in demand from the late Teens through the Forties and best
known for the many features in which she played opposite Will
Rogers. On radio, she was always sponsored from 1933 through
1944 by Welch's Grape Juice, appearing in a variety of 15-minute
dramatic series. In 1934, for example, Irene Rich portrayed Lady
Margo Carstairs off to Australia to locate her supposedly dead
husband, while in 1936 she was a lawyer. The program originated
at the NBC Chicago studios, and on Irene Rich's forty-second
birthday, October 13, 1933, Welch's hosted a party there which
anyone was invited to attend. *Variety* (May 29, 1934) quite rightly
noted, "As a radio personality she is probably without counter-
part." **185. Harry Richman** (1895–1972). Harry Richman's
chief claim to fame, as far as radio is concerned, is that he introduced payola to broadcasting, when in the early Twenties he
accepted money from publishers to sing their songs on WHN-
New York. A song-and-dance man and also an accomplished
composer ("Singing a Vagabond Song," "Walkin' My Baby
Back Home," etc.), Richman was a favorite on radio for many
years.

185

186

186. Dick Powell (1904–1963). *The New York Times* (January 4, 1963) described Powell as "a phenomenon of show business," an accomplished star of film musicals and drama, a director, head of his own production company—Four Star Television—and a radio performer. Powell's many radio programs included *Hollywood Hotel* (CBS, 1934–1938), *Your Hollywood Parade* (NBC, 1937–1938), *Campana Serenade* (NBC, CBS, 1943), *The Fitch Bandwagon* (NBC, 1944), *Rogue's Gallery* (Mutual, 1945) and *Richard Diamond, Private Detective* (NBC, ABC, 1949–1952). **187. Robert Ripley** (1893–1949). Robert Ripley first introduced his *Believe It or Not* newspaper cartoons in 1918, and transferred the idea to radio, on NBC, in 1930. Ripley and *Believe It or Not* were heard almost continually from then onward either as a separate program or as part of a variety series, on NBC, CBS and Mutual. In 1939, Ripley had the distinction of having his show in New York sponsored by Royal Crown Cola, despite Royal Crown's being unavailable in the city. He is seen here with Ozzie Nelson (See No. 168).

187

188

1626-41

188. Roy Rogers (1912–   ). Fresh from his film triumphs at Republic Pictures as the King of the Cowboys, Roy Rogers came to radio with his own show on the Mutual network in November of 1944. With him on the show, which was later heard on NBC, were the Sons of the Pioneers (until 1948), Foy Willing and the Riders of the Purple Sage (post-1948) and, from the mid-Forties onward, Rogers' second wife, Dale Evans. The happy trails of *The Roy Rogers Show* came to an end in 1955. **189. Will Rogers** (1879–1935). Will Rogers, the nation's philosopher-hero, used radio much as he had earlier used his vaudeville act and newspaper column, to comment on the vagaries of American life and society. Rogers' best-known program was *The Gulf Show,* which began on NBC in 1933, and was to be heard on CBS up to the time of the entertainer's tragic death.

190. President Franklin Delano Roosevelt (1882–1945). The thirty-first president of the United States (1933–1945) was perhaps the first president to realize the potential of radio for promoting his government's policies. Through his "fireside chats," Roosevelt attempted to "sell" America the New Deal and his other major programs; all of the president's greatest speeches were on radio, from the first, on March 4, 1933, "the only thing we have to fear is fear itself," through the last, on March 1, 1945, "I am confident ... we can begin to build, under God, that better world." Eleanor Roosevelt was also a frequent broadcaster but, unlike the president, she had a sponsor. **191. Baby Rose Marie** (1923–   ). Rose Marie Curley won a beauty contest at the age of three, the prize for which was a trip to Atlantic City, where she was invited to appear on station WPG. Rose Marie's first major radio appearance was on WJZ-New York in July of 1931 and *Variety* (July 28, 1931) had to admit, "No doubt about the child having talent and an exceptional voice and delivery." It was that adult voice which gained Rose Marie her own 15-minute show on the NBC-Blue Network the following year, on which she promoted Julius Grossman Shoes. At the age of 12, Rose Marie retired, but returned to show business in 1947 and has since been seen on television on *The Dick Van Dyke Show* (1961–1966) and *The Hollywood Squares* (1968 to date). She never seems to be inactive. **192. Lanny Ross** (1906–   ). Lanny Ross, a delightful tenor with an engaging smile, was first heard on radio on December 24, 1928, and was soon known to listeners as the Troubadour of the Moon. Ross became an instantaneous success as a result of his appearances on the Maxwell House *Show Boat* (NBC, 1932–1937). The singer remained a radio favorite through the Fifties, starring in such shows as *The Packard Hour* (CBS, 1937), and, in addition, had a successful Hollywood career, starring in *Melody in Spring* and *College Rhythm* (both 1934). He is also a composer of note.

190

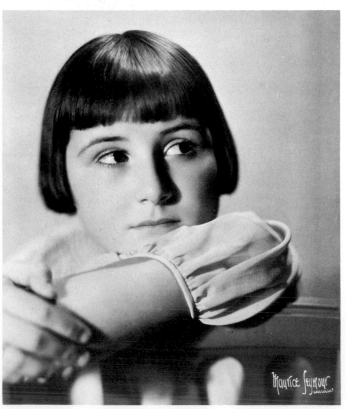

191

192

193. **S. L. Rothafel** (1882–1936). Samuel Lionel Rothafel, better known as "Roxy," was one of the great theatrical showmen of his day. He transformed his key New York theaters, the Capitol, the Strand, the Roxy and Radio City Music Hall, into national showcases. His broadcasting career began in 1923 when he was heard on *The Capitol Family Hour,* broadcast from the stage of the Capitol Theatre. He used the broadcasts, which featured the theater's stage show, to promote audience attendance there. From 1927 through 1931, Roxy presented *Roxy and His Gang* on the NBC-Blue network. **194. Dave Rubinoff** (1896–). Billed as simply Rubinoff and, aside from Jack Benny, radio's best-known violinist, Dave Rubinoff began his professional career in 1912. He made his radio debut in 1931 with Eddie Cantor, with whom he remained for a number of years. A serious illness forced him off the air, but Rubinoff returned to the NBC-Blue network in the summer of 1943, after a five-year absence, with a program entitled, appropriately enough, *Rubinoff Returns.* **195. Harry Rose** (circa 1892–1962). A burlesque comedian who began his career in 1910, Harry Rose was a somewhat effeminate master of ceremonies in vaudeville and on radio, rather similar in manner to the young Jack Benny. He was also noted for his appearances on television's *Colgate Comedy Hour.*

193

195

194

201

201. Kate Smith (1909–   ). A giant of radio, both physically and artistically, Kate Smith came to the medium in 1931, after a number of years on the stage and after Columbia Records representative Ted Collins had taken her under his wing. For that first broadcast, on May 1, Kate Smith adopted what was to become her signature tune, "When the Moon Comes Over the Mountain." Soon her opening and closing greetings, "Hello, everybody!" and "Thanks for listenin'," had become the best known on CBS. She was heard almost continually on that network, under the sponsorship of A & P, General Foods, Grape Nuts, Sanka and others, through 1949, when she signed with ABC for one year. Later she was heard on Mutual, and, of course, was a frequent performer on television until her retirement in 1979. Of the singer who introduced—on November 11, 1938—"God Bless America," President Roosevelt once said, "This is Kate Smith. And Kate Smith is America." **202. Ann Sothern** (1909–   ). An attractive comedienne and singer in Hollywood films of the Thirties and Forties, Ann Sothern came to radio in the summer of 1945 with a series based on her popular *Maisie* films, produced by M-G-M. The radio program ran concurrently with the production of the films and was a foretaste of the delight

Miss Sothern was to be on television in *Private Secretary* and *The Ann Sothern Show*. **203. Whispering Jack Smith** (1898–1950). Jack Smith, the Whispering Baritone, began his professional career singing with a vaudeville quartet in 1915; in 1918 he joined the Irving Berlin Music Company as a song plugger. Smith became popular on radio in the late Twenties and at the same time became a Victor recording star. In the Thirties, Smith was to be heard on a 15-minute program on WABC, sponsored by Ironized Yeast. *Variety* (August 4, 1931) commented, "He has ether personality and a masculine virility decidedly different from that of the average pop singer." After a hiatus in the late Thirties, Whispering Jack Smith was back on radio in 1941 with an early morning show, three times a week, on WEAF-New York. **204. Phil Spitalny** (1890–1970). Phil Spitalny organized his first all-girl, 22-member, orchestra in 1933 after many years with an all-male group. Spitalny and the orchestra were the stars of the long-running *The Hour of Charm,* heard sometimes on CBS and sometimes on NBC from 1935 through 1948. Spitalny married Evelyn Kaye, known professionally as "Evelyn and Her Magic Violin." (Peggy Ryan is also seen in this still from the 1945 Universal film *Here Come the Co-Eds.*)

202

WISPERING

Vitaphone #216

203

204

99

210

211

210. Ed Sullivan (1902–1974). A *New York Graphic* and later *New York Daily News* columnist, Ed Sullivan was first heard with an interview show on CBS in 1932, and continued on radio through the Forties. His program, *The Toast of the Town,* received its premiere on CBS television on June 20, 1948, became *The Ed Sullivan Show* in September of 1955 and left the air in 1971. Sullivan's success on both radio and television was due entirely to his guests, for, as Fred Allen once said, "He will last as long as someone else has talent."   **211. John Charles Thomas** (1889–1960). John Charles Thomas, famed baritone of opera, concert platform and radio, made his professional debut in 1912, and soon gained immense popularity, particularly with women, thanks to his rich, powerful voice and his fine features and athletic build. The singer made his radio debut on WJZ in August of 1931; he was a regular on many programs, including *The Ford Sunday Evening Hour* (CBS, 1936–1937) and *The Pause That Refreshes* (CBS, 1940–1941). Between 1943 and 1946, Thomas had his own 30-minute Sunday program for Westinghouse on NBC.   **212. Gladys Swarthout** (1904–1969). A good-looking and temperament-free opera star, Gladys Swarthout made her debut at the Metropolitan in 1929. She helped to popularize opera on radio in the Thirties and Forties, being featured regularly on such programs as *The Palmolive Beauty Box Theatre* (NBC, 1934) and *The Prudential Family Hour* (CBS, 1941–1944). Miss Swarthout retired in 1956.

220. James Wallington (1907–1972). James Wallington made his radio debut on WGY-Schenectady in 1924; he joined NBC in 1930 and became one of its top announcers, best remembered for introducing Roosevelt's fireside chats. In 1966, Wallington joined Voice of America and remained with that organization almost until his death. **221.** Harry Von Zell (left) and Don Wilson. **Harry Von Zell** (1906–1981). Harry Von Zell probably had the greatest following enjoyed by any announcer thanks, largely, to the many years he spent on radio and television with Burns and Allen. He obtained a firm foothold on radio in 1929 when he became announcer for Paul Whiteman, and was later to be heard on shows with Eddie Cantor, Bing Crosby, Phil Baker, Stoopnagle and Budd, and Dinah Shore, among others. Late in his life, Harry Von Zell was well known to California television viewers as the spokesman for Home Savings and Loan. **Don Wilson** (1900–1982). Don Wilson began his career with KFEL-Denver in 1923 as a singer, later moving, in 1929, to KFI-Los Angeles as an announcer. He resigned from NBC in 1934 to join Jack Benny and remained with the comedian for the next 33 years. ("I guess I laughed in the right places," he suggested once as the reason for his longevity with Benny.) In addition to working with Jack Benny, Don Wilson could also be heard on such programs as *Glamor Manor* (ABC, 1944–1947). (See also Introduction figure.)

220

221

222

222. Rudy Vallee (1901–   ). Not only was Rudy Vallee one of radio's greatest stars, he was also one of its greatest starmakers. When Vallee came to network radio, on NBC, in 1929, his greeting of "Heigh-ho, everybody!" was already familiar to New York nightclubgoers. The Rudy Vallee program, known back then as *The Fleischmann Hour,* provided 60 minutes of unique Vallee talk, jokes and music, and also introduced a gallery of well-known names to broadcasting, including Eddie Cantor, Noel Coward, Beatrice Lillie, Alice Faye, Edgar Bergen and Red Skelton. In 1940, Rudy Vallee introduced John Barrymore as a regular on his program, and the great actor remained with Vallee through 1942. When Vallee joined the U.S. Coast Guard in 1943, his show went off the air, but returned in 1944, and as late as the Sixties, Rudy Vallee was still to be heard on local radio.

223

223. Orson Welles (1915–   ). The man responsible for two of the greatest classics of the cinema, *Citizen Kane* and *The Magnificent Ambersons,* learned his craft on radio in the Thirties on such programs as *The Cavalcade of America* (NBC), *The Columbia Workshop* (CBS) and *The March of Time* (NBC). *Les Misérables* (Mutual, 1937) and *The Shadow* (CBS, 1937–1938) followed, and then came *The Mercury Theatre on the Air* (CBS, 1938–1940) with its infamous *The War of the Worlds* broadcast. Other Orson Welles programs include *Orson Welles Theatre* (CBS, 1941–1943), *Ceiling Unlimited* (CBS, 1942–1944) and *This Is My Best* (CBS, 1944–1945).

224

224. Fred Waring (1900–). One of the best-known orchestras on radio from 1933 onward, Fred Waring's band was described by *Variety* (December 4, 1935) as "one of the most imitated on the ether. ... More concert than anything else, with pop tunes for the adolescents and choral arrangements for the rocking chair crowd." Waring started on CBS, where he adopted his signature tune, "Breezin' Along with the Breeze." He moved to NBC in the late Thirties, on which network his best-known programs were *Chesterfield Time* (1939–1944) and *The Fred Waring Show* (1945–1950). Today, Fred Waring and His Pennsylvanians are still a popular featured attraction, despite Waring's no longer being able to lead the aggregation. **225. Jack Webb** (1920–). Many of the television series and films with which Jack Webb is closely associated had their origins in earlier radio programs featuring the actor-writer-producer. Webb could be heard on *One Out of Seven* (ABC, 1946), *Johnny Madero, Pier 23* (Mutual, 1947), *Jeff Regan, Investigator* (CBS, 1948–1949), *Dragnet* (NBC, 1949–1956) and *Pete Kelly's Blues* (NBC, 1951).

225

226

227

226. Ted Weems (1901–1963). Leader of one of the popular bands on radio in the Thirties and Forties, Ted Weems was noted for whistling a song and then inviting the audience to whistle along. His style of music was similar to that of Lawrence Welk, which made it perfect for the NBC musical quiz *Beat the Band,* heard from 1941 through 1943. **227. Paul Whiteman** (1890–1967). One of the best-known orchestra leaders of the twentieth century, Paul Whiteman became a national figure after his 1924 initial presentation of George Gershwin's *Rhapsody in Blue*. Whiteman was very active on radio, being the first star of *The Kraft Music Hall* on NBC in 1933 and hosting such programs as *Paul Whiteman Presents* (NBC, 1943) and *The Radio Hall of Fame* (NBC-Blue, 1943–1945). In 1947, he became a disc jockey on ABC with his own Monday-through-Friday program.

228

229

228. Marie Wilson (1916–1972). Marie Wilson first became the world's stereotypical dumb blonde in Ken Murray's *Blackouts,* a Hollywood revue from 1942 through 1949, in which Miss Wilson never missed a performance. She brought her dumb-blonde characterization to radio with *My Friend Irma,* which was to be heard on CBS from 1947 through 1954. **229. Meredith Willson** (1902–   ). Before he wrote *The Music Man* and following his years as a flutist with the New York Philharmonic,

Meredith Willson was providing the music for many popular radio programs, including *Carefree Carnival* (NBC, 1933–1935), *Good News* (NBC, 1937–1940). *Coffee Time* (NBC, early Forties) and *The Big Show* (NBC, 1950). For the last, Willson composed "May the Good Lord Bless and Keep You" for Tallulah Bankhead to sing at the show's close, and always acknowledged Miss Bankhead's introduction with "Thank you, Miss Bankhead, sir."

230

231

232

230. Walter Winchell (1897–1972). From a child vaudeville performer with Gus Edwards and a prominent newspaper columnist, Walter Winchell graduated to radio performer in July of 1930 with his own 15-minute program on WABC. *Walter Winchell's Journal* was first heard on the NBC-Blue network in 1932 and ended its days on ABC in 1955. Winchell would always commence his program with a shouted greeting to "Mr. and Mrs. North America and all ships at sea." On June 28, 1937, Winchell starred in *The Lux Radio Theatre* production of *The Front Page*. "Poor Walter," Dorothy Parker once remarked. "He's afraid he'll wake up some day and discover he's not Walter Winchell." **231. Charles Winninger** (1884–1969). Charles Winninger had played Captain Andy in the original 1927 New York production of *Show Boat*—and was to essay the role in the 1936 film version—so it was not unnatural that Winninger play Captain Henry on the Maxwell House *Show Boat* on NBC from 1932 through 1934 and again in 1937. **232. Tony Wons** (1891–1965). Tony Wons was radio's poet-philosopher of the Thirties, reading sentimental verse and dispensing homilies on *Tony Wons Scrapbook* (first heard on CBS in 1930) and *The House by the Side of the Road,* accompanied by Ann Leaf at the organ. His perennial greeting was "Are yuh listenin'?" Wons retired in 1943.

233

234

233. Alan Young (1919–   ). Born in Great Britain and raised in Canada, Alan Young made his screen debut in 1946 and around the same time embarked on a career in radio. He was heard on *The Jimmy Durante Show* (CBS, 1948) and on *The Texaco Star Theatre* (CBS, 1947, and ABC, 1948) before commencing his own program, for Tums, on January 11, 1949. Probably Young's biggest success to date has been on television in the *Mr. Ed* series on CBS from 1961 to 1965. **234. Robert Young** (1907–   ). In films since 1931, Robert Young entered radio in the mid-Thirties, and among the series on which he was heard are *Good News of 1939* (NBC, 1939) and *Passport for Adams*

(CBS, 1943). Of course, Young is best known for *Father Knows Best*, first heard on NBC on Thursday, August 25, 1949, under the sponsorship of General Foods, and a popular radio program through 1954. **235. Ed Wynn** (1886–1966). Ed Wynn was a vaudeville and revue comic who evolved into a fine screen character actor, and along the way was heard frequently on radio, beginning with a WJZ broadcast in 1922 of his stage hit *The Perfect Fool*. Wynn is best known for the title role of *The Fire Chief*, the Texaco-sponsored program that began on April 26, 1932, but he was later heard as *The Perfect Fool* and on *Happy Island*.

235